A Suffolk Nature Diary

To FRANCES & JONATHAN

Trevor

MAY 2013

by Trevor Goodfellow

Printed and Published by

Leiston Press Ltd

Unit 1b Masterlord Ind Est

Leiston Suffolk

IP16 4JD

Tel: 01728 833003

Email: glenn@leistonpress.com

www.leistonpress.com

ISBN

978-1-907938-54-2

Foreword

With my passion for wildlife photography, I was inspired by a man who took a daily photograph of his children growing up. My original idea was for a daily single point photograph throughout the year but this evolved into a diary format recording the different species of fauna seen throughout the year with over 500 photos.

Each season presented its own challenges to successfully produce a faithful 'photo-a-day' record of flora and fauna on site here at a 30 acre former dairy farm in Suffolk.

Weather and opportunity dictated the quality of these images along with the normal challenges associated with wildlife photography. I did the best I could under these conditions.

I learnt a lot from writing my first wildlife diary in 2010. This book relates to the year 2012, including a few notes on 2011 below.

I find it is fascinating to look at the diary each year, to compare key events like: the first swallow or frogs spawning and I hope that this diary gives the reader as much pleasure and interest in the biodiversity here, as it did for me compiling it.

Trevor Goodfellow

Acknowledgments

Thanks to the following experts for their help and advice:

Rob Parker	Butterfly Conservation (butterflies)
Peter Maddison	Butterfly Conservation (butterflies)
Tony Prichard	Butterfly Conservation (moths)
Adrian Chalkley	Suffolk Naturalist Society (freshwater invertebrates)
Patrick Barker	Barn Owl ringing
Adrian Knowles	Insects
Adrian Parr	British Dragonfly Society
Steve Barnes	Quiet Sports (fish netting)

And
www.ukmoths.org.uk
www.britishbugs.org.uk
Suffolk Wildlife Trust
British Trust for Ornithology (BTO)

Notes about 2011

It was a strange year, weather-wise: hot dry April up to 30 deg C, a late frost and an official drought, ending with a mild and mainly dry autumn.

The moat dried out by May and was still dry into December. This meant that the newts didn't spawn and the ruddy darter dragonflies had no opportunity to hatch.

Despite the lack of any ruddy darters, young newts, or carp spawning, I did record twenty species of butterfly although in low numbers.

The late frost caught many freshly sprouting plants including the walnut tree which lost its first crop of nuts. Conkers appeared bigger this year despite the effects of leaf-miner grub.

I managed to photograph the purple hairstreak butterfly for the first time ever and also photographed orange tip and brimstone.

A major find was a rare male common blue aberration which attracted interest from the British Entomological Society and Butterfly Conservation Group.

With help from friend Paul, a massive bramble clearing project was launched. The pond known as 'King's Pond' across the large hay field was renovated and water plants transplanted from the lake. We also cleared the ditch behind the lake which was quickly filled with various common and unusual wild flowers.

The weather and fish overcrowding caused there to be no weed and the grass carp ate everything green they could reach. But I finally managed to get the lake netted in October and sold 876 lb of fish, among which there were three small grass carp and one large at 19 lb 8oz. about 300 small perch were removed and a surprise 2 lb 3oz perch was caught at the charity match we had on the 29th October. The winning weight was only 28 lb 1oz, an overall total of about 100 lb but these remaining fish should benefit substantially in health and growth now. Indeed the fish fattened up well going in to the winter.

In late autumn, signs of kestrel, little owl, barn owl and tawny owl were among the birds preparing for spring. I noted skylarks, robins, blackbirds all singing away in October!

Newts and a hedgehog were still showing on wet nights up to 30th December.

As the weather eventually cooled down the birds flocked to the feeders: greenfinch, goldfinch, siskin, chaffinch, brambling and a single sighting of a tree sparrow, first noted. Redwing and fieldfare flocked in smaller numbers than 2010.

It will be interesting to see how the trees recover from significant restoration, particularly the Plane and Holm oaks.

January

Jan 01 2012. (11degC. Showers) SR-08.04 hrs SS-16.00 hrs

A mild fine morning turned wet and overcast by noon. Fish feeding well and water level up to just above the pipe. Owl pellets on the floor in the cart lodge prompted me to erect wildlife camera in the rafters to help with i.d. Tonight the lone hedgehog is still foraging under the bird feeders. Woodpeckers, jays (jan1), siskin, and finches still flocking in.

Jan 02 (5degC. Dry)

Fine day mostly sunny with cool breeze. Fish still feeding, I caught a 6 lb mirror known as 011, it looked fit and fat. Moles are avoiding the traps and continue to make a mess. Great tits and treecreepers noticeably calling. Still no water in the moat although the lakeside ditch is holding some water (jan2a). Some toothed fungi near owl oak (jan2b).

Jan 03 (6degC. Heavy rain)

High winds and heavy showers (jan3) cleared to give a sunny afternoon but still windy into evening. Ditch and lake took a few centimetres of rain and King's Pond up as well (jan3b). New planting is looking good too. Kestrel was busy hunting.

Jan 04 (8degC. Windy)

Still blustery through the night but dry. Fish are off the feed, water clearing slightly. Iris and bee orchids are peeping through now. On return home I saw a short-eared owl for the first time. Variegated Holly 'silver queen' looks pretty (jan4) and a fragrant blossom on a garden shrub (jan4b).

Jan 5

Jan 5a

Jan 6

Jan 7

Jan 05 (7degC. Changeable)Very high winds up to 60mph, not surprising that the climbing frame blew over. Photo Jan5 shows the waves made by these winds. Hens sheltered in the barn most of the day (jan5a). Clouds cleared p.m. and winds dropped at dusk. Half moon shines brightly and possible frost tonight.

Jan 06 (6degC. Sunny)

Lovely fine day with bright sun but cool. Wind dropped to about 10 mph or so giving me the chance to clear up the twigs blown off the willows. With help, I put the Jungle Gym back up after being upturned by the recent gales. Photo opportunities for finches and a quick snapshot of a siskin on the niger seed feeder (jan6). Robins looked like they were getting territorial and gangs of long tailed tits happily played in the thicket. Still a few hares on the hay field and shooting nearby hopefully thinned out the partridge which steal the chicken's food. The wild flower seeds I ordered have arrived now, so I must find a suitable position to sow them. Sanfoin and Birdsfoot trefoil were chosen as these are food plants of common blue and other butterflies. Daffodils shooting up around the thorn tree outside the window, nice. Pruned gelder roses near the gate and found several ladybirds.

Jan 07 (8degC. gusty winds, Dry)

Very cold winds and occasional bright sun. Missed a photo opportunity this morning, a bird took off from the lake which resembled a cormorant but was likely to be a black throated diver. I later found three small dead perch in the margins; could the bird have killed them and not fancied eating them? A lone fieldfare fed on the last few crab apples hanging on the tree (jan7) and crows mobbed a kestrel near the paddocks. I caught two common carp about 6 lb which gave a good fight.

Jan 8b

Jan 9a

Jan 9

Jan 08 (8degC. Fine)
Kestrel watched for prey from the top of the Turkish hazel tree (jan8) then hovered over the meadow. I did a bit of fishing and caught another 6 lb common carp, fish were feeding well again. Only a couple of chaffinches but the usual flocks of greenfinch and goldfinch. A pair of jays and magpies were first to the feeders this morning. Several hares on the hay field were chasing about and mating (jan8b). Occasional bright sun was very nice which helped me get a nice photo of a female siskin.

Jan 09 (9degC. Fine)
Full moon last night (jan9), with a halo! Not easy to photograph the halo though. Fieldfares on the crop in the next field and a few siskins showed. A short morning fishing session gave me two takes on the leger, both were take-and-run which is unusual; one was 6 lb and the other nearly 8 lb, lovely (jan9a). Strimmed around the lake and cleared some of the weeds on 'Oak Hill'.

Jan 10b

Jan 10

Jan 10 (8degC. Fine)
Last night a hedgehog was out and about. From the surveillance camera (on TV) I watched a bat flying around the barn and this morning I found that the nature cam had recorded of a pair of barn owls wooing in the barn roof, excellent. Heron and a pair of mallard lakeside at first light. Morning stroll revealed evidence of an otter kill (jan10b), common carp about 5 lb or more. Robin, blue tit, great tit and blackbirds all busy and noisy. At dusk, a barn owl balanced on a cane to spot its prey (jan10).

Jan 11 (10degC. Fine)
Bright night in the waning moon last night made for a comfortable 'otter patrol'. No sign of him but several little owls called to each other. I noticed some dandelions in flower by the roadside and flag iris are shooting up. Early daffodils are making the most off the mild weather and continuing to grow taller. Moat is still dry and looks unlikely that the lilies there will survive this year. Female siskin looked pretty in the sun (jan11). A quick fishing session with maggot for perch before dark was a success (jan11a)

Jan 11

Jan 11 a

Jan 12

Jan 12a

Jan 12 (9degC. Changeable)

Cool stiff breeze spoilt the odd sunny spells. Spotted woodpecker on the peanuts in the afternoon. Grey squirrel gave me the slip so no pic. Animal droppings near the ditch, compiled of mostly rabbit hair, probably fox's (jan12), lay in characteristic prominent position, on a tuft of grass. I am planning to build a new owl box soon to try to encourage the barn owls closer. I also put two more tit boxes up (bought ones but they were cheap). Large fungi near lake have lasted a long while and seem frost resistant (jan12a).

Jan 13 (4degC. Fine)

Frosty morning after 2 deg C last night. A sunny and fair, but chilly day. A small flock of Siskins were feeding on the small cone like seeds on the alder trees. Through the condensation on the window I photographed a green woodpecker (jan13). Barn owl flew out of the right hand oak by the lake and hunted for a while at dusk. I checked the owl box in the barn to find a small round egg, first guess was: abandoned stock dove but I thought I would check my books as a barn owl egg is similar. Reckon I was right, barn owl egg is a tad larger. Several dunnocks around and large numbers of crows in flocks (jan13a) (a murder or parliament of crows).

Jan 13a

Jan 13

Jan 14a

Jan 15

Jan 14

Jan 14 (4degC. Fine)
Mainly sunny and calm (jan14a). Still no sign of any bramblings but about 20-30 siskins were chattering away in the large oak with eight or more joining blue tits and goldfinches (jan14) for a drink from the ditch. Great tits and long tailed tits were showing along with green woodpecker and greater spotted woodpecker. A pair of wrens frantically chased around the lake margins while robins sang merrily.

Jan 15 (2degC. Fine)
Lake froze last night with the freezing point reached (jan15). Ice receded by afternoon enabling a short fishing session until light failed at 16.15 hrs. I caught two fish: one about 2 lb and the other 9.7 lb in the net. Lots of partridge loitered on the drive as they went to roost.

Jan 16a

Jan 16b

Jan 17a

Jan 16 (3edegC. Fine)
Ice on the lake thickened and a white frost covered the grass. Barn owl was successfully hunting just before dusk (jan16a) while I stumbled on a pair of goldcrests (jan16b) in the holm oaks, illuminated by the orange setting sun . Fieldfares have discovered the Pyrocantha berries near the barn and steadily devouring them.

Jan 17 (2degC. Fine)
Well below freezing last night. A morning cacophony of birds ready to leave their roosts made up of flocks of greenfinch and goldfinch. These were accompanied by flocks of siskins and a nice surprise: a song thrush. A few more chaffinches today and a few lapwings flew over around lunchtime (jan17a). A pair of Yellowhammers were a welcome sight (jan17), sunbathing in the top of a tree near the pool house. Moles are being a pest and managing to tunnel even in frozen ground. Blackbirds and fieldfares competed for the remaining berries on offer.

Jan 18 (4degC. Rising to 9. Showers)
Rain laid on the icy lake until it thawed by lunchtime. I disturbed a sparrowhawk at the feeders in the afternoon. Finally built and erected a barn owl box in the cart lodge (jan18) spurred on by signs that they had been back in the night.
Jan 19 (9degC. Fine)
A few short showers with sun, wind gusty after dusk. About lunchtime, hundreds of finches and siskins were singing away in their roost by the ditch, I couldn't see many as they were well concealed. Sparrowhawk flew past the feeders again. The red Dogwood is quite striking (jan19).
Jan 20 (5degC, Wet & windy)
Dreary day with up to fifteen hares played on the large hayfield. A song thrush avoided a photo call and later, a pair of mallard landed on the lake. A cock chaffinch had a siesta after a good feed (jan20a).

Jan 18
Jan 19
Jan 20a

Jan 21 (7degC. Wet & windy)
Rain overnight raised the ditch water a couple of inches (jan21a). A coal tit appeared on the feeders and a few more chaffinches too. Cheeky french partridge (jan21), several rob the chicken feed in the mornings.

Jan 22 (9degC. Windy)
Sunny intervals helped the make the day bearable. Wind blew the feeders onto the ground and the lake was very 'choppy'. Bright orange fungus on willow stump (jan22).

Jan 21a

Jan 22

Jan 21

Jan 23a

Jan 25

Jan 23

Jan 23 (5degC. Fine)

Breezy but sunny most of the day. Spotted woodpecker was drumming on the old oak (jan23) and after work I fished for a while until about 16.15 hrs when it got too dark, didn't catch anything but had a few knocks. I know the fish were feeding as I gave them a few pellets in the morning. A pair of wagtails (jan23a) searched for food together, always nice to see and hear them. A few robins, singing and feeding. (jan23b).

Jan 24 (5degC. Rainy)

No moon last night and a beautiful starry sky! 1 deg C. I counted at least thirty goldfinches, twenty greenfinches and around twenty chaffinches, two of which were lame with a scaley leg: a mite problem. A few siskins etc joined in the feeding frenzy. Three collard doves (jan24) strutted about gracefully.

Jan 25 (5dgeC. Overcast)

Chilly and calm. Fifteen hares in the large field about five of the chasing about. A heron landed in the field but a long way off (jan25). Birds emptied the feeders by lunchtime and a large flock of finches scattered when two Apache helicopters flew low overhead. Moat is still damp although rain is forecast which should start to show in the bottom. I was told that yesterday's pic of robin which I sent to ITV weather, was featured on TV. Looked like lots of tiny flies floating on the lake appeared dead, some in flight also.

Jan 23b

Jan 24

Jan 26

Jan 27

Jan 28

Jan 26 (5degC. Showers)
Heron fishing at first light and lake is murky suggesting the fish are feeding prompted by a slight rise in pressure and temperature. Magpies were noisy under bedroom window collecting fallen birdseed from a feeder. Bitterly cold wind made a short fishing spell uncomfortable but sunny spells were nice. Caught about six fish up to 6 lb some quite chubby but all were fit and well. A bit of a stand-off as three robins met up while the bird table was busy (jan26).

Jan 27 (5degC. Fine)
After a wet start the sun shined for the rest of the day with blue skies. 30-40 fieldfares fed on the pasture and many different bird songs could be heard throughout the day. A short fishing session before dusk was fruitful, giving four fish: 2.5 lb tench, two 8 lb common carp and a 6.6 lb mirror known as' number 10' (jan27) which weighed 3 lb in 2007.

Jan 28 (3degC. Fine)
Three blue tits seemed to be in a 'discussion' about ownership of a nearby nest box (jan28), as they investigated the box. Chaffinches unsuccessfully tried hanging on to use the feeders. I think I heard a willow warbler this morning although several blackbirds were singing and occasionally distant songs were deceiving. I came in from a short fishing session at 16.30 hrs, just getting dark. Recent rain has created a small puddle in the moat where I dug up a lily last year.

Jan29 (2degC Fine)

Foggy start to the day with a frost (0degC). Some mallard were on the lake at first light and a finch-onslaught on the feeders as usual for a cold morning. Fine but must be the coldest day for a while, birds singing –they don't mind. (jan29).

Jan 30 (2degC. Showers)

Dusting of snow after a freezing night (jan30). Three swans probably hooper swans, flew overhead towards Nether Hall and masses of finches emptied the feeders again.

Jan 31 (1degC. Fine)

Fine snow flurries last night and this morning but generally fine but cold. As usual, many birds flocked to feeders and some feathers seemed like evidence of a sparrow hawk attack. The maize belt in the next field hosted large numbers of carrion crows, jackdaws and rooks (jan31). Both spotted and green woodpeckers were about. Song thrush (jan31a) appeared again, nice.

Jan 31

Jan 30

Jan 29

Jan 31a

February

Feb 2

Feb 3

Feb 3a

Feb 01 (SR 07.39 hrs SS 16.30) (1degC Fine)
Frosty night left ice on most of the lake for
the rest of the day (feb1). Barn owl hunted
successfully, early on and many siskins
appeared again. Brisk breeze meant that most
birds (including hens) sheltered from the cold.
Feb 02 (1degC Fine)
Lake froze last night when temperatures
dropped to -3 or 4. Spotted Woodpecker (feb2)
fed on the peanuts in the sun. Many finches
are finding a drink in the ditch. Frosty grass
stayed white in the shade. A few moorhens
have appeared to look for food and a pair of
pied wagtails look like they are 'coupled up'
ready for spring.
Feb 03 (1degC. Fine)
Cuckoo pint and Bee orchids are shooting up
and Daffodils are 'on hold'. A few blackbirds
(feb3a) gathered in search for food. On the
way home last night I saw two barn owls
between Tostock and Thurston. Lots of hares
again, chasing about (feb3).

Feb 6d

Feb 4

Feb 6

Feb 6a

Feb 7

Feb 6c

Feb 6b

Feb 04 (1degC. Cloudy)
Well below freezing last night and the lake now has between 25 – 50mm of ice. Overcast but forecast is for a few inches of snow tonight. Stiff cold westerly breeze made for a tough day. A family of long tailed tits (feb4) was a welcome sight.

Feb 05 (0degC. Cloudy)
Over 10cm of snowfall overnight (feb5). 'nature-cam' captured a roe deer before snow covered the camera. Hundreds of hungry birds feeding. It is a struggle to maintain a drinking bowl for them in these conditions. Even more chaffinches than yesterday. A few floating gooey algae blobs frozen into the lake's surface (feb5a) but insignificant compared to 2010/11 maybe netting the lake has improved the general balance. I noticed where I walked, some bluebells are pushing up under the snow.

Feb 06 (0degC. Fine)
A little snow overnight followed by a rise to 1degC. Hens still haven't ventured out of the coop. lots more tracks in the snow today (feb6c) as deer, rabbits and hares search for food. More cock chaffinches than hens and finally a half decent pic of the hen chaffinch (feb6). A wren poked in gaps in the snow drifts against the flint wall and long tailed tits (feb6a), fieldfare (feb6b), green woodpecker and siskin showed. Lots of animal tracks in the snow, notably deer, rabbit and hare. And other strange signs like two 25mm holes with no tracks.

Feb 07 (1degC. Sunny)
Crispy after overnight frost on the thaw of yesterday. Barn owl was out in the afternoon and even more 'unidentified running objects' tracks. 'Jenny' wren (feb7) was obliging for a photo too. I have put nature-cam out to try to establish what is making tracks on the drive, otter and fox or stoat. As the sun went down, temperature plummeted to well below freezing.

Feb 8a

Feb 9

Feb 10a

Feb 08 (2degC. Fine)
Below freezing overnight (feb8a) and a full moon making it seems like just a cloudy day.
Result! First picture of a tree sparrow (feb8). Two came to the feeders and stayed for the
morning at least. They also found the millet feeder which they really liked. Jays, blackbirds
and a song thrush scrapped for food and a few siskins battled the other finches for prime feeder
space.

Feb 09 (0degC. Overcast)
A dead rabbit that I placed near the nature-cam was gone this morning and fox tracks
nearby. On inspection, I found that I had forgotten to replace the memory card! So no
pics of Mr Fox. Another new arrival on the feeders was a Coal Tit (feb9). Tree sparrows
returned. Spotted woodpeckers drumming in all directions, one used the tit-box for this. Eight
blackbirds and a total of eighteen species of birds just at the feeders. A grey squirrel gave me
the slip so no photo of him.

Feb 10 (0degC. Fine)
Snipe and woodcock flew up in the car headlights on the long drive late last night, unusual
to see them at the same time but very much winter visitors. A rook, partridge and pheasant
sneaked in for a feed and the siskins happily fed on the niger seed. Woodpeckers were going
from nest box to nest box (feb10a) hammering away, sounded like machine-gun fire. Frozen
grass looked like fireworks (feb10).

Feb 8

Feb 10

Feb 11

Feb 12

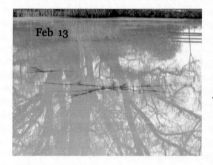

Feb 13

Feb 13a

Feb 14

Feb 11 (-1degC. Fine)

Minus 9 degC this morning (feb11) but the sun 'warmed' things up. More strange tracks in the snow and it's now difficult to distinguish them as everywhere is covered with footprints. No sign of the sparrows today but a pair of spotted woodpeckers got together and the barn owl hunted at dusk (17.15hrs)

Feb 12 (3degC. Fine)

Minus 5 last night and foggy this morning. Grass is beginning to show through the snow a lot more as a gently thaw occurs and the icy surface of the lake appears wet (feb12). This morning I watched a few siskins at close quarters, their singing was so pretty.

Feb 13 (3degC. Showers)

Minus 1 degC last night. A pair of tawny owls were 'toowit-toowooing' after dark. The thaw on top of the icy lake refroze overnight and is thawed again though still 50mm of ice I guess. The ice is opaque which highlights the strange star shaped patterns (feb13). Rain has washed away most of the snow revealing more bluebells (feb13a).

Feb 14 (5degC. Changeable)

Chilly but at least the snow has gone, bar a few small patches. The ditch has a good deal more water in it just from the thaw (feb14). Signs that the barn owl has been in the cart lodge so I have put the nature-cam out again. 'wonky' hen is very poorly and despite attempting to eat, has difficulty balancing. I might have to 'deal with it' in case it isn't old age but viral, shame as she is the tamest of them all. Early daffs are in bud.

Feb 18a

Feb 15

Feb 17

Feb 18

Feb 15 (8degC. Windy)

Lake ice is 99% thawed and water is cloudy suggesting that the fish may have come on to feed and a small amount of floating 'algae' has accumulated. Sadly 'wonky' the tame hen had to be put down today. On a lighter note some snowdrops are showing (feb15) on the moat side.

Feb 16 (8degC. Fine)

Cool breeze made it feel colder today but good light in general, helped photography. Flocks of fieldfares and a few redwings showed along with a visit from Mr & Mrs Mallard. Cuckoo pint leaves are unfurling now and a few more bulbs. A good sunset ended a fair day at about 17.45 hrs. (feb16)

Feb 17 (9degC. Breezy)

Dry day with wind chill. Two short fishing sessions: early morning and late afternoon, were fruitful with a few small carp and one about 5lb along with the big tench at 2 – 3 lb. (feb17). A solitary moth was attracted to the outside light last night and daytime saw several gnats and small spiders. A stock dove investigated a hole in the right oak prospecting for a nest site. This hole is or at least was home of the squirrel.

Feb 18 (9degC. Windy)

First crocus in bloom (feb18a). I persisted with fishing this a.m. but it became too windy, although I did catch 'polly' a common carp about 7 lb. (feb18).

Feb 19 (5degC. Fine)
Cold breeze and sunny afternoon. Caught a nice mirror carp just before dusk, '016' on the list at 5.5 lb, was 2.7 lb in 2008. Just as I was writing this entry I saw Barny out hunting so I dashed out with the camera. It seemed like there were two but I returned as one took a vole back to the nest hole. Hares were chasing about like it's spring (feb19a). Mallard have been in-and-out (feb19). Run out of bird seed again.

Feb 20 (5degC. Fine)
Cool breeze after below freezing last night. A little ice on the lake quickly thawed during the morning. I discovered lots more crocus in bloom and others not quite in bud. The birds seemed very pleased that I refilled the empty feeders as they massed in flocks in the large oak trees this afternoon, singing away. Blue tit (feb20).

Feb 21 (11degC. Fine)
Frosty start to a mild day cooled by a stiff breeze. A skylark rose in the sky singing while I photographed a redwing (feb21) and a dozen starlings merged with a flock of forty or more fieldfares.

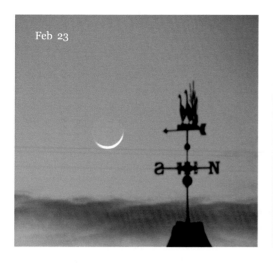

Feb 23

Feb 24

Feb 22 (10degC. Windy Showers)
Spotted woodpeckers were chasing each other and great tits and blue tits were getting fruity and investigating the nest boxes. A muntjac snuck across the paddocks. Robins, dunnocks, tits and finches were all calling and singing.

Feb 23 (14degC. Fine)
Windy but sunny day birds think it's spring. Woodpeckers drumming, blue tits looking in nest boxes and more crocuses appeared. Little owls and barn owl calling and bats flying at dusk, unable to i.d. (feb23).

Feb 24 (12degC. Fine)
Newts appeared near the flint wall last night both crested and smooth (feb24 & 24a) a swan flew over, it looked a bit dirty. Several flies and a few bees emerged from hibernation and a couple of male winter moths were attracted to the outside light in the evening, the females of this species are flightless (feb24b).

Feb 24b

Feb 24a

Feb 25 (7degC. Fine)
Another dry day with a chilly breeze. A couple of cheeky rooks raided the feeders first thing. Kestrel and sparrow hawk showed themselves and about one hundred fieldfares were around most of the day finally going to roost at dusk. A final short fishing session around 17.00 hrs disturbed the barn owl which went back in to his nest hole. Little owls called to each other throughout the day. Hens were a bit more lively today having fun scrapping and dust bathing, first eggs for several weeks were produced today. Cock pheasant shone in the sun (feb25).

Feb 25

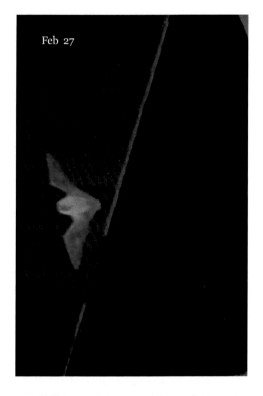

Feb 27

Feb 27b

Feb 26

Feb 27a

Feb 26 (10degC. Fine)
Tried to find where the little owls roost but no result so I have put nature-cam out tonight watching a post which has a lot of spraints on and near it. Only small fish bighting throughout the day. Another rook scrounged scraps near the feeders (feb26) and kestrel hunted this morning. Just caught site of the barn owl returning to roost mobbed by crows.
Feb 27 (11degC. Overcast)
Bats out again last night (feb27) and white splashes on the front gate and drive may indicate an owl was about later. More crocuses (feb27b) and early tulips showing too. Great tit was again interested in a nest box (feb27a).

Feb 28 (11degC. Fine)
Heron flew up from the bench swim early a.m.
hundreds of fieldfares, redwings and starlings
flocked. Twenty Brent geese flew over noisily
just before dusk when Little owls and barn owl
showed. I saw one tiny pipestrel bat just after
sunset. Dunnock (feb28).

Feb 29 (13degC. Fine)
Two magpies were patrolling the lakeside this
morning which made me think that the mild
spell had lured toads from their hibernation.
I couldn't find any evidence of dead toads but
sure enough, I did here a toad croaking later
on. Some fish were jumping and a few were
surfacing to feed on some fish food. Again,
starlings, fieldfares and redwings gathered in
their hundreds. Barn owl hunted after sunset
and the little owls defied my attempts to
photograph them and only showed after sunset
when light was too poor. I did however get a few
shots of a buzzard which flew overhead (feb29).
A flock of siskins joined in with the cacophony
of bird song early p.m. lesser Celandine spotted
in flower (feb29a).

Feb 29a

Feb 28

Feb 29

March

Mar 2

Mar 1

Mar 1a

Mar 1b

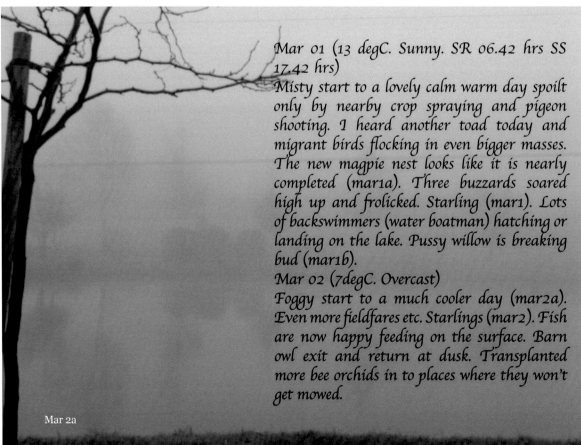

Mar 2a

Mar 01 (13 degC. Sunny. SR 06.42 hrs SS 17.42 hrs)

Misty start to a lovely calm warm day spoilt only by nearby crop spraying and pigeon shooting. I heard another toad today and migrant birds flocking in even bigger masses. The new magpie nest looks like it is nearly completed (mar1a). Three buzzards soared high up and frolicked. Starling (mar1). Lots of backswimmers (water boatman) hatching or landing on the lake. Pussy willow is breaking bud (mar1b).

Mar 02 (7degC. Overcast)

Foggy start to a much cooler day (mar2a). Even more fieldfares etc. Starlings (mar2). Fish are now happy feeding on the surface. Barn owl exit and return at dusk. Transplanted more bee orchids in to places where they won't get mowed.

Mar 3a

Mar 3

Mar 4

Mar 4a

Mar 03 (11degC. Changeable)

Today had rain 'written all over it' but despite some black clouds, the sun shone for a while. First frog sighted and a surprise visit from a pair of grey lag geese (mar3a). I set some wild flower seeds namely greater birds' foot trefoil and sanfoin which are both food plants of several butterfly caterpillars. I startled a kestrel lucky I had my camera (mar3). At least three little owls with competing calls at dusk.

Mar 04 (7degC. Showers)

Finally some rainfall which I shall measure tomorrow. Dwarf tulips are up but not budding yet and snakes head fritillaries that I plated yesterday have all been munched by deer. Starlings still increasing in numbers and rooks, jays and pheasants invaded the feeders this morning. Great tit (mar4). Just before sunset the temperature dropped from 7 to 3 deg C and rain turned to snow! (mar4a).

Mar 5

Mar 05 (4degC. Showers/Gales)
Temp dropped to 1 deg C last night and very windy. A few puddles about now. A heron patrolled the lake margins at dawn and then later in the afternoon (mar5a). Even more starlings gathered on hay field (mar5) and as I write this, several tiny long-tailed tits feast on the fat balls.

Mar 5 a

Mar 6b

Mar 06 (7 degC. Fine)
20cm of rainfall recorded over the last two days, the ditch water is up (mar6a) and some water in the moat now (mar6d). King's Pond is also high (mar6). Several ladybirds (mar6c) and a few gnats and bugs about. A lovely dwarf iris (mar6b) has bloomed in my garden and the other irises are growing quickly. The Gunnera has survived the winter and is sprouting two new leaves. The lake looks messy as masses of small rafts of goo floated to the surface, hopefully tomorrow's forecasted rain will break it up.

Mar 6a

Mar 6c

Mar 6d

Mar 6

Mar 7

Mar 07 (7degC. Rain)
A couple of dead fish on the bank could be heron kill as one certainly had harpoon damage but it was missing it's head, maybe cat dog or fox. I disturbed a little owl while checking the fallen oak in advance of cutting and moving it, and thought I saw an owl in a hole in the standing part of the tree but on return with my camera, it was an optical illusion. Strange purple 'toadstools' turned out to be aquilegias and violets (mar7) are plentiful around the emerging bluebells. First wood anemone (mar7a) by the lake.
Mar 08 (7degC. Fine)
Frosty morning and an early stroll surprised the rabbits (mar8). I saw a bumble bee today, the sun was shining but very cold breeze took the edge off it.
Mar 09 (10degC. Fair)
One Muscovy Duck (mar9) landed early a.m. but wasn't keen on staying when it saw me, later it returned and seemed a bit more settled, each time it only flew as far as next door. A fresh algae bloom on the lake looks messy. Early daffs are now open and blackthorn buds are swelling. Five rooks and a magpie (mar9a) raided the feeders; four fat balls disappeared since last night.

Mar 8

Mar 7a

Mar 9

Mar 9a

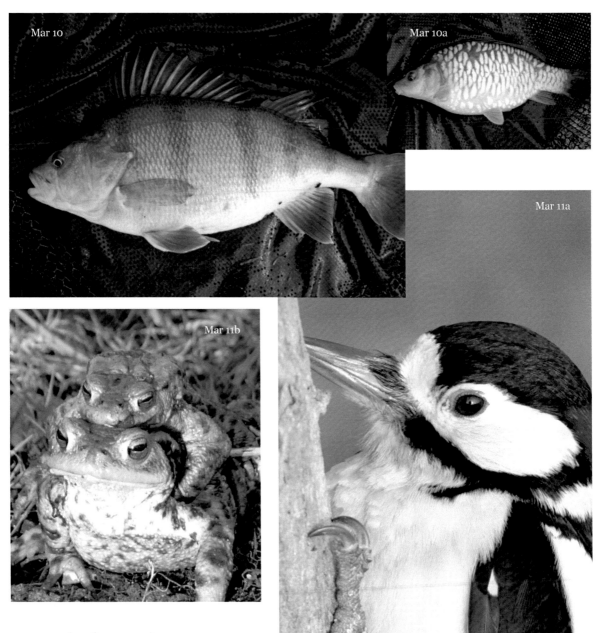

Mar 10

Mar 10a

Mar 11a

Mar 11b

Mar 10 (12degC Fine)

Early fishing session scored a Perch weighing in at 2 lb 7 oz. (15 inches long. Mar10) also a nice but small, fully scaled mirror carp (mar10a). Pieces of moss and grass around the pool house door are signs that the blue tits are nesting in the porch roof again. A few little croaks from toads and I think I saw one trying to climb onto the duck island. A few siskins remain and a small number of fieldfares.

Mar 11 (12degC. Sunny)

A bang on the bedroom window early a.m. was down to a greater spotted woodpecker (mar11a) which rested on a tree trunk with its head hanging over onto its back. When I went to check, he had revived and eventually flew away. A few toads (mar11) are in the newly exposed ditch so I hope the water stays long enough for them to breed. Muscovy duck visited a couple of times. A bit of croaking going on and some toads coupled up (mar11b), also sounds of the gruff croaking of frogs but unable to see any. Several various geese flew over at dusk. Water hawthorn is in bloom.

Mar 12

Mar 12 (11degC. Overcast)
Misty start to a cooler than the forecast, but OK day. More beautiful dwarf irises (mar12) have appeared in the garden and hawthorn is starting to bud. I pruned the dogwood this afternoon as leaves were starting to form. At dusk, a Canada goose snuck in without me noticing until too dark to photograph. A little owl flew ahead of the car as I drove along the avenue. Only about 20-30 toads spotted while on walkabout about after dark.

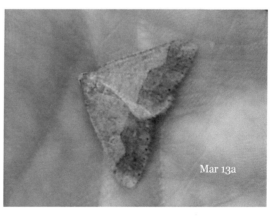

Mar 13a

Mar 13 (12degC. Overcast)
Flag irises are growing quickly and umbrella grass marginals are showing new growth. I found a small moth faking death which turned out to be a dotted border (mar13a). Heron visited a couple of times and fish happily fed on floating pellets. Finally got a rat (mar13) near the hen house, possibly poisoned although maybe Ziggy excelled herself. On a quick inspection after dark, I counted over 80 toads, many paired up. Not as mild as the forecast today.

Mar 13

Mar 14d

Mar 14c

Mar 14b

Mar 14

Mar 14a

Mar 14 (7degC. Fine)
Average day weather-wise, though very eventful; a young mute swan (mar14d) greeted me on my return at lunch, two pairs of bullfinches (mar14c) were attracted by the budding blackthorn and yellowhammers (mar14) and linnets (mar14a) arrived along with some reed buntings (mar14b). Later on the sun came out for a while I took about 150 photos today and really only a few are worth keeping or showing here. Chickens are still laying well some days there are 3 – 5 eggs.

Mar 15 (14degC. Sunny)

Misty start to a warm sunny day. Fish weren't biting but kestrel and buzzard soared above while spring like things went on at ground level. Quite a number of croaking paired-up toads and sightings of reed buntings. Blue tits are nesting in the box near the bedroom window and they are making a noise at this moment. A queen wasp, several bumble bees, gnats and a pair of small tortoiseshell butterflies in the garden. A pair of green finches had a bath in the ditch (mar15).

Mar 15

Mar 16 (11degC. Overcast)

Chilly breeze in the morning. Lots of yellow hammers and a few reed buntings still. A pair of bullfinches was too shy for a photo. A pair of Mallard are still loitering, pulling up marginals and damaging plants. About 20 pairs of toads just near the bridge which is a favourite shallow place for them to spawn in the reviving water mint. Last night four or five crested newts and a smooth newt were out looking for food but not ready to migrate to spawning waters yet it seems, although the forecasted rain tomorrow might bring them out if it is mild enough. A brisk stroll after dark revealed over 200 toads plus spawn and 2 frogs, no newts along the flint wall so I will inspect the moat tomorrow. Fish feeding (mar16).

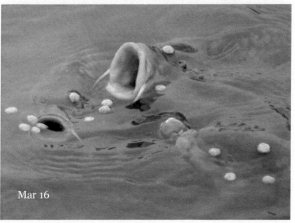

Mar 16

Mar 17 (9degC. Wet)

Many paired toads spawning and 5 frogs, 2 small clumps of frogs spawn (mar17). Several yellowhammers but they are a bit shy to get a good photo. Female Sparrow hawk flew over the lake after being mobbed by crows.

Mar 17

Mar 19

Mar 20a

Mar 18

Mar 18 (7degC. Showers)

Possibly a dozen reed buntings, mostly female (mar18). Too many toads to count now and a lot of toad spawn strings. Tonight I counted 10 frog spawn clumps.

Mar 19 (10degC. Fine)

Frosty start and cool breeze made it cold when the sun went in. finally photographed the little owl (mar19). A buzzard flew low but tree got in the way so no pic. A pair of shelduck thought about landing on the lake just before dusk. I counted 11 frogs and as many clumps of frog spawn. Hens are still laying well and being a nuisance by hanging around the front door (mar19a). Pied wagtails about but no evidence of nest building yet. A long tailed tit struggled with a large feather so maybe they are nesting.

Mar 20 (12degC. Sunny)

Cool start and some clouds. Two grey lag geese were perched in the top of the old oak, very strange. Very spring like what with bumble bees (mar20), daffs and lots of croaking. Bird song throughout the day including skylark. Lovely display of violets near the henhouse (mar20a). Dwarf tulips have opened but forgot to photograph so I hope the deer don't eat them tonight.

Mar 19a

Mar 20

Mar 21

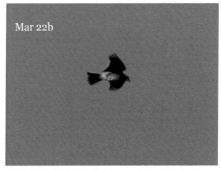
Mar 22b

Mar 21 (14degC. Sunny)

Toad exodus has begun but still a hundred or so spawning etc. I also counted 11 frogs. An early morning stroll around the meadow turned good as I spotted a pair of goldcrest in the conifers and yews (mar21) very fidgety but a better photo than earlier this year. Pied wagtails are interested in the barn I guess they have chosen a nest site. Mallard duck are causing a lot of floating debris as they pull marginal plants and other vegetation.

Mar 22a

Mar 22 (15degC. Sunny)

After a night of only 2degC the day was surprisingly fine. Last night a bat skimmed the lake surface in the misty glow of the outside light, could be a daubentons bat. 15 frogs counted today and coincidently 15 lumps of frogs spawn. First sound of the chiffchaff lured me to the front gate with my camera (mar22a). Lots of bees and bumbles feeding on the flowering goat willow. Sky larks sang as they rose out of view (mar22b). A lone female toad strolled up the drive towards the lake in the afternoon sun. both ditch and moat are starting to dry up with no sign of rain for another few days.

Mar 23 (17degC. Sunny)

After a very cold night about 4 deg C, the day warmed up lovely. There are still toads spawning and frogs guarding their spawn. The fish sun bathed at the water surface and a bit of leaping occurred throughout the day. The goldcrest gave me the slip this morning and a call on my mobile phone messed up a possible close up of the yellow hammers. My new camera lens arrived today and as it has a larger aperture; it was very different from my regular long lens. Might get a chance tomorrow if it isn't dark when I finish work. Lots more wood anemones and some more tulips are in bud. Later on I caught the large tench weighing in at 2 lb which is down a bit (mar23b). A pair of mallard flew over (mar23).

Mar 23b

Mar 23

Mar 24a

Mar 24b

Mar 25

Mar 25a

Mar 24 (18degC. Sunny)
Another cold night and misty morning. The sun brought out a peacock butterfly from hibernation (mar24b). Pied wagtails (mar24a) very busy jostling for the right to mate I think. Still more toad spawn and 16 frog spawn. Several bunnys about in daylight. Hedge cutting was completed today just in time for bird nests and blossom. During the sweep-up I stumbled over a tree creepers nest where the adult birds were frantically in and out so I assume they have chicks. I will try to photograph tomorrow.

Mar 25 BST (15degC. Sunny)
Sticky buds are opening (mar25a) and the fish were sunbathing. I saw the tree creepers but they didn't show at the assumed nest site. In the lane I spotted some lovely pinky white violets (mar25). Pumped some lake water into the moat to help the newt survival.

Mar 26a

Mar 26b

Mar 26 (16degC. Sunny)
I discovered this morning that the tree I was watching for a tree creeper, was the wrong one. I surveyed the right one and it paid off (mar26a). Patience also paid off in the search for the chiffchaffs and willow warbler (mar26b). I rescued a red tailed bumble bee (mar26) from the water and sighted a comma and a large white butterfly. Two large birds flew high over, I think they were cormorants.

Mar 26

Mar 27a

Mar 28a

Mar 27c

Mar 27 (18degC. Sunny)
Warm and calm after an over night frost. Followed chiffchaff, tree creeper and barn owl (mar27a) today and just missed little owl and snipe. Plenty of bugs including wasp, bee, gnat, crane fly and a comma butterfly (mar27b). A few fieldfares are still about and a thrush sang merrily at dusk. At least five small bats feasted on the bugs after sunset pipestrels I think (mar27c).

Mar 28 (20degC. Sunny)
Calm warm day after 2degC overnight. Frog and toad spawn is hatching (mar28a) and many different bugs are in flight. A squirrel in the left hand oak (mar28b) has started building a dray. I saw a white butterfly and two commas. About a hundred fieldfares were feeding on the large hay field. At dusk a number of geese flew over and the day ended with a nice sunset.

Mar 28b

Mar 27b

Mar 29

Mar 29 (19degC. Sunny)
Cool breeze in the afternoon. A few more queen wasps (mar29b) emerged from hibernation in the shed and several various bumble bees (mar29c) looked for nest sites and a few bee-flies (mar29) drank moisture from near the ditch with their long proboscis.

Mar 30 (15degC. Fine)
I went to Pensthorpe nature reserve in Norfolk for a trip out today but I saw these two grey lag geese on the lake first thing (mar30).

Mar 29c

Mar 29b

Mar 30

Mar 31d

Mar 31c

Mar 31 (10degC, Overcast)

Cold wind with a few spots of rain. Blackthorn (mar31d) is just catching up with surrounding trees and is now blossoming. Two grey lags were on the lake early a.m. again. While fishing, a stoat ran by and when I returned with my camera I had a few quick glimpses (mar31e). Some pied wagtails were making a lot of noise which alerted me to a passing sparrowhawk. The native bluebells (mar31c) are in flower also the magnolia (mar31b). Cute little yellow toadstools caught my eye (mar31a).

Mar 31a

Mar 31e

Mar 31b

April

Hail Stones

Apr 2b

Apr1b

Apr 1

Apr 2

Apr 1 (12degC. Fine)
Cool breeze for a while after 4 degC over night. Tried photographing a black cap which soon
gave me the slip, but tree creepers were quite unbothered about me at close quarters. Tulips
are opening (apr1) and daffs are coming to an end (apr1b).

Apr 2 (10degC. Fine)
Another very cold night and a chilly breeze came with the sun. By chance I found a pond
snail (apr2), which is great to see, as I introduced a handful summer 2010 never really
thinking that they would survive. Clematis on the wall is in full bloom (apr2b).

Apr 3 (11degC. Showers)
Fine morning but clouding over later with showers. Great tits (apr3) are nest building in a dead elm by the lane. No sign of the blackcap today. The dray high in the left hand oak is looking more like a carrion crow's nest, although I haven't seen any building materials delivered. While the sun shone, I spotted a strange beetle (apr3b) (Silpha rugosa). A small tortoiseshell kindly landed in the sun for a few snapshots (apr3c). Rooks are still raiding the feeders and this morning they unhooked the fat-ball feeder and stole a couple of them breaking the lid on impact with the ground. I heard a whitethroat and blackcap but saw neither. A lovely big bumble bee stayed still for a pic too (bombus terrestris, queen) (apr3d).

Apr 4b

Apr 4a

Apr 4 (10degC. Showers)
About 20mm of rain in the last 24 hrs
(apr4b) this revitalised the ditch and
raised the lake by about that amount.
A stiff breeze all day turning northerly.
I watched two goldcrests early – before
it rained, but poor light robbed me of a
good photo (apr4a). Reed mace has shot
up from appearing dead two days ago to
20 - 30cm. (apr4c)

Apr 4c

Apr 5b

Apr 6b

Apr 6a

Apr 6c

Apr 5 (10degC. Changeable)
Five grey lag geese on the lake at dawn looked like they were competing for a mate. Also some indication that they were checking out nest sites in the marginal plants. Pied wagtails and great tits seen with nest building materials. The wind fallen black poplar stump is sprouting nicely (Apr5); I think it is the only one we have. A sparrow hawk flushed birds from the feeders and even spooked a pheasant. Ladybird (apr5b).

Apr 6 (10degC. Sunny/Showers Full Moon)
0degC and frost overnight, icing up the ditch water but sunny blue skies by 09.00 hrs. At King's Pond, the water level is good after rain and one lot of frog's spawn is beginning to develop (apr6a). Several lily pads have surfaced (apr6c) on the shallow planted ones including the fringed lily. Pied Wagtails still nest building (apr6b).

Apr 5

Apr 7 (8degC. Fine)
Very cool breeze but some sun. Water hawthorn is blooming well (apr7). At 17.40 the sky was still bright after sunset.

Apr 8 Easter Sunday (10degC. Showers)
It is now noticeable that most trees are in leaf or at least breaking bud apart from the oaks which are a bit behind the ash at the moment. A toadstool growing from a rotting branch (apr8a) could be peeling oysterling.

Apr 9 (9degC. Showers)
The black seed heads of the sedge are quite striking as they contrast against the fresh green leaves. Quite windy and very wet. A very clean cock blackbird posed today (apr9).

Apr 10a

Apr 10b

Apr 11

Apr 11c

Apr 11b

Apr 10 (11degC. Fine)

Breezy start calming at dusk. Kestrel hunted over hay field in the afternoon. Willows and other trees are even greener now. I found a grub, possibly a crane fly larva (apr10a) seemed to have suffered an attack of some kind maybe a parasitic fly. Under a bush by the ditch, I saw a broken egg shell of a thrush, hopefully due to nest clean-up, not predation; two halves so probably a hatched one. More water-born insects hatching from the water's surface. Lesser celandine show is peaking (apr10b).

Apr 11 (10degC. Showers)

Wavy Bittercress (apr11c) is just coming into flower, always just at the water's edge, maybe seeds are spread by floating. A female orange tip butterfly (apr11) settled in the garden and later I spotted a male. Primroses have bloomed and a few cowslips in the meadow (apr11b). Some poo around lake and elsewhere are signs that hedgehogs have emerged. I had a walk late at night but no sign of any.

Apr 13

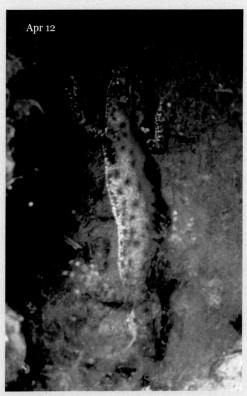

Apr 12

Apr 14a

Apr 14b

Apr 12 (9degC. Showers)
Only a couple of millimetres of rain in the last two days but at least there is still water in the ditch as I saw a male crested newt after dark last night (apr12) also a few smooth newts, females of which still looked like they were holding on to spawn till milder days. I heard a black cap but still no sighting. I watched goldcrests for a while and got a few nice snapshots.

Apr 13 (10degC. Showers)
Barely a millimetre of rain after a foggy dawn when a few grey lag geese popped in again. I heard the blackcap again but no pics. A pair of mallard are still hanging around (apr13).

Apr 14 (9degC. Changeable)
Breezy morning after another cold night. I finally spotted the blackcap (apr14b) but only managed a dodgy pic as light failed and he wouldn't show himself lower in the blackthorn trees. Also saw the treecreepers again and a chance spotting of a small leopard slug, about 7cm long, in the cart lodge (apr14a). They do grow to 15cm. FIRST SWALLOW.

Apr 15

Apr 16a

Apr 16b

Apr 17

Apr 15 (8degC. Changeable)
Blackcap and bullfinch (apr15) amongst the blackthorn and pied wagtails fed on bugs hatching from the grass in the sunny spells.

Apr 16 (8degC. Changeable)
Dry day but cool. Cut some grass today, it was lush. A ground beetle (apr16a) hitched a ride in the wheelbarrow when I carted a load of dandelions. Blackcaps still very shy but I heard them again and spotted a male and a female. I have yet to i.d. a strange appearance on some lakeside nettles (apr16b) looks like eggs of some sort but in fact, I find that it is nettle rust fungus.

Apr 17 (max11degC. Fine)
Another very cold night with high winds. A bit of morning rain, followed by sunny intervals. Tadpoles (apr17) have reappeared and are looking well.

Apr 19

Apr 19b

Apr 20b

Apr 20

Apr 20a

Apr 18 (8degC. Showers)
Cool and windy day and the usual rooks raiding the feeders. Trees are looking green now, rowan is showing buds as are many trees. (apr18).

Apr 19 (10degC showers)
A robin is building its nest (apr19b) in the cart lodge. I hope Ziggy doesn't find it! A few more fungi have appeared, notably the tiny brown cowpat toadstool (its yellow. Apr19). First pondskater seen on the water's surface in the moat. Thalia delbata is showing new leaves and the marsh marigold now has five leaves, I hope it blooms; this is now its second year, previously getting damaged by ducks and grass carp. After dark I checked along the flint wall and found at least four crested newts. This explains why I have only found one male in the ditch; they seem to be waiting for milder weather before moving to water.

Apr 20 (9degC. Wind/Showers)
Black clouds missed us on both sides but a short hailstorm and rain and drizzle was 'nice'. A pair of grey lags (apr20) called in for a swim and wreck the plants. Fish loved the bread (apr20a) donated by the sandwich shop and I spotted several large carp feeding in the margins downwind and one of them was huge, could be a double! The strange common horse-tail plant (apr20b) is showing at the lakeside. 13mm of rain.

Apr 21 (8degC. Showers)
Dry spells with thunder storms late afternoon. We had a major dandelion offensive today. The broody hen is still sitting on the donated eggs: quail, blue hen, and pheasant, from a week or two ago. At least nine hares chased around the large hay field. Green woodpecker appears from time to time but very shy. I managed to photograph a female blackcap, between showers (apr21).

Apr 22 (12degC. Showers)
Cool breeze and very cloudy at times. I stumbled across a strange common morel toadstool (apr22) supposed to good to eat. The new addition to the 'arboretum' is a Monkey puzzle tree planted on the far side of the meadow.

Apr 23 (7degC. Wet)
Two Canada geese called in and tested the duck island early a.m. (apr23b). Some colourful toadstools sprung up near my foxgloves (apr23a) and a couple of green shield bugs were on a wild mullion plant in the garden (apr23c).

Apr 26

Apr 24 (10degC. Showers)
Much the same as yesterday; stiff breeze. I spotted a
brown lipped snail in the grass, quite common but pretty
(apr24). Three Swallows skimmed the lake for a drink at
about six o'clock and large grass carp nibbled the reeds
at dusk. 21.15hrs: I just heard a barn owl outside the
window.

Apr 25

Apr 25 (8degC. Rain)
Wet and windy, ditch is wet the full length (apr25) and
lake is up another inch or so. Grass is need of another cut
as the recent rain has had a massive effect on growth. Grey
lags popped in again this morning and late afternoon I
saw five more that thought about landing. Thousands of
tadpoles are now visible again.

Apr 26 (12degC. Gales)
It's April alright! Sun and rain (apr26). Grass is growing
like mad and dandelions burst out everywhere when the
sun comes out. A male Sparrowhawk swooped by the
feeders and still, the rooks unhook the feeders before I get
up in the morning. After dark, two hedgehogs snorted and
courted near the bird feeders (apr26a).

Apr 26a

Apr 24

Apr 27 (11degC. It's April!)
A few rumbles of thunder and occasional rainbow. At first light, a female tufted duck swam on the lake and later a pair of English partridge (apr27) ran from under the bird feeders. Late afternoon I heard the FIRST CUCKOO. A couple of pond skaters seen on the lake and the ditch.

Apr 28 (6degC. Wet n Windy)
The tufted duck (apr28) was back again this morning and apart from a glimpse of jays and green woodpecker, I stayed in indoors most of the day.

Apr 27

Apr 28

Apr 29 (11degC. Showers)

20mm rain since 20th April. Considerable surface water with puddles and waterlogged grass. Ditch is up about 100mm and lake is 12cm clear of the bridge. Several more green shield bugs on the mullion. At the garden centre, I treated myself to two swan mussels and two ramshorn snails (apr29) for the lake.

Apr 30 (14degC. Mainly Fine)

Breezy with storms in the distance after dark. Rain has filled ditch to the top of the small stepping stone (apr30) and water has collected in the ditch near the main gate.

May

May 3a

May 3b

May 3

May 1b

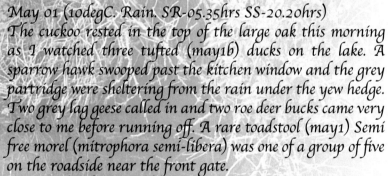
May 1

May 2

May 2b

May 01 (10degC. Rain. SR-05.35hrs SS-20.20hrs)
The cuckoo rested in the top of the large oak this morning as I watched three tufted (may1b) ducks on the lake. A sparrow hawk swooped past the kitchen window and the grey partridge were sheltering from the rain under the yew hedge. Two grey lag geese called in and two roe deer bucks came very close to me before running off. A rare toadstool (may1) Semi free morel (mitrophora semi-libera) was one of a group of five on the roadside near the front gate.

May 02 (12degC. Fine)
Grey partridge are happy here, I see them several times a day. I strimmed around the lake and cut most of the grass. The lake is still high: only a few centimetres off the bottom edge of the bridge (nearly to the top of the drain pipe). Ditch is about full (may2b). Two green woodpeckers (may2) fed on the cut grass and I spotted a pair of Goldcrest. Several bees had fallen in the lake so I managed to rescue a few. The broody hens are sitting tight and sharing the incubation of the blue egg which should hatch soon.

May 03 (8degC. Wet)
Thunder storm last night showed 36mm in the rain gauge. This amount of rain filled the ditch (may3a), raised the lake to above the pipe and now the water is touching the bridge (may3). The moat also looks more 'normal' at about two thirds full (may3b).

May 4

May 5

May 6

May 7a

May 7c

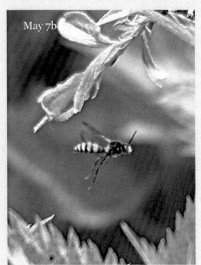

May 7b

May 04 (8degC. Wet)
Field drainage is topping up the moat via ditches, and maybe this water drains to the lake as there is overflow under the Monet bridge and then to the ditch and onwards towards the fallen oak. The kestrel has been hunting mostly over the garden. At the end of the moat I spotted two bunnies in the entrance to their nursery burrow, as I found out later, splashing noises proved that it had flooded. A few pond skaters chased a swarm of small gnats on the water's surface as the levels still rise. The purple tulips are finally coming to an end and the cowslips in the meadow are still doing well. Both apple and crab apple are in blossom now. Cuckoo pint seemed very slow to flower but here is the first I have seen this year that hasn't been eaten by deer (may4).

May 05 (8degC Dull)
Cool and breezy day. A lot of surface water has now drained away. Bog bean is in flower (may5) and sedge is too.

May 06 (9degC Drizzle)
Started to pollard a lakeside willow in the afternoon, still a bit to do. Strange eggs on 'hoary plantain' (may6) possible caddis fly. These eggs are laid in one mass so I assume the plant stem has grown and segmented them.

May 07 (10degC. Wet/sunny intervals)
Tracked down a Whitethroat (may7a) and when the sun came out, it highlighted several solitary bees and various flies around the brambles (may7b, digger wasp). Red coloured cuckoo pint (lords & ladies) showed near the ditch (may7c).

May 8

May 9

May 08 (14 degC. Fine)
Cloudy start and breezy but some sun later. A pair of Tufted ducks again and Mr Heron. A jackdaw probed for food (may8). The fluffy seeds are blowing from the goat willows and tadpoles are ravenous as they work their way around the lake eating algae. A few swallows skimmed the lake as they swooped about but no sun so no pic. Just a rabbit when the sun did shine.

May 09 (14degC. Rain)
Two very fat crested newts were still near the flint wall last night. Tadpoles are prevalent and some are being eaten by carp but it is hard to tell weather this is accidental or not. Drizzle most of the day but the mild temperature is making the fish lively. Another strange fungus has appeared near the front gate (may9) possibly a cauliflower fungus. I cleaned out hens coop to find that a quail had hatched but died, probably trampled.

May 10 (16degC. Rain)
Milder but drizzle most of the day. I spent a day at a Suffolk Wildlife Trust talk then on to their Grove Farm (about half a mile away) with the view to be one of their flora recorders. A pair of grey partridge was feeding near the gate as I returned. Grey heron (may10).

May 10

May 11b

May 11

May 12

May 11 (14degC. Fine)
Very windy. Grass has grown since Wednesday 9th and all is very lush. I chipped the willow cuttings, some of which had started to root into the ground! During a sunny interval this afternoon, I followed a blackcap along the lane and stumbled across a speckled wood butterfly (may11). May blossom is out on some bushes (may11b).

May 12 (16degC. Sunny)
Whitethroat and blackcap have been giving me the run-around today and I managed to get better pics of chiffchaff instead. Great spotted woodpecker, song thrush, lesser whitethroat, a pair of tawny owls and a pair of grey partridge graced the day. Pied wagtail (may12) seemed to be still nest building. After dark, as I suspected several bats: Soprano pipestrels fed on the masses of gnats and flies that hatched today.

May 13b

May 13 (16degC. Sunny)
A baby Robin (may13b) watched me as I photographed a thrush with a beak full of worms. I found out why some carp were very keen to feed near the surface in a small area near the bridge; thousands of small fry (may13), likely to be perch have hatched and apparently tasty if you are a fish. Swallows loved all the flying bugs and a swift joined them at one point. Finished pollarding a lakeside willow, wow it was quite tall and we had to drop it in the water to avoid squashing nearby trees. Tit box near the feeders was busy and so too the great tits in the box near the farm house back door. One orange tip male and a holly blue represented the butterflies today.

May 14 (10degC. Wet)
In the morning a heron (may14) stalked the lakeside where I feed the fish, it struck and stumbled into the water and leapt out empty handed (empty mouthed?). A jay joined the other crows on a scavenger hunt and many other birds were also busy singing and feeding their young. Horse chestnut is in bloom, both red and white. A nice surprise as I went outside at sunset to see two pairs of tufted ducks happily swimming about the lake and several swallows swooping around, while I photographed these, a Little owl settled in the hedge by the lane.

May 15 (9degC showers/hail)
Windy with some sun. I went to a 'dingy skipper' survey today in the king's forest. We saw a few butterflies but no skippers. Germander speedwell (may15) and wall speedwell are in full bloom and quite eye-catching for a tiny flower. The grey partridge preened and fed just outside the bathroom window (may15b) photos turned out well considering they were taken through rain drenched double glazing.

May 13

May 14

May 15

May 15b

May 16a

May 18

May 16 (11degC fine)

I managed to cut the grass as it was quite lush and now need to start to plan for the froglet exodus. A crane fly rested on the front door (may16b) but tricky to photograph, notice the wing counterbalance pendulums. Ziggy has found the robin's nest in the barn and has just stolen a chick. I managed to rescue it and replace it but not sure what will happen now. I have tried to protect the nest access with wire. A few solitary bees (may16a) (maybe mason bees) investigated the barn structure. A couple of swifts were flying over head but didn't stay.

May 17 (12degC. Fine)

This morning I tried to photograph the barn owl hunting, when a pair of Egyptian geese (may17) surprised me, they flew off for a while and returned to rest in the owl oak for a while. The owl (or two) caught two voles which were taken to the nest, so good news. One orange tip male and another white butterfly showed.

May 18 (15degC. Fine)

Pleasant day turning to showers after sunset. Barn owl is still successfully hunting for voles, another two this morning. The grey partridge are still about and several jays and jackdaws looked for food on the freshly cut lawns. The tadpoles are quite big and appear all around the lake. The bright sun and mild temperature only lured a couple of butterflies: an orange tip and a white of some sort, although I though I saw a female brimstone I couldn't confirm that. A few swallows (may18) about but they haven't investigated the barn for nesting yet.

May 17

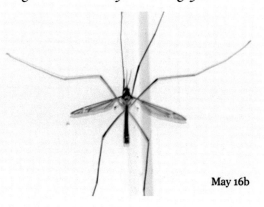

May 16b

May 19

May 20

May 22

May 21

May 22b

May 19 (15degC. Fine)

Showers over night but dried out quickly. Broad leaved thorn is in bud and most rowans are in flower, though the Hupeh rowen is dawdling. A lovely tuft of sedge is in flower and the seed heads look like caterpillars. A Buzzard wheeled over head while a small spider on vetch in the meadow captures a beetle for dinner (may19).

May 20 (12degC. Fair)

Cool breeze but otherwise dry. I tried the moth trap last night but only caught one moth! An ermine moth (may20). Crows are a pest raiding the feeders still.

May 21 (12degC overcast)

Windy and cool. A hedgehog appeared in my headlights on return last night. Jays, jackdaws and rooks are raiding everything including any bread in a bag left out for the fish. A French partridge seemed poorly and allowed me to get really close (may21). Ziggy left a mouse on the doorstep for me this morning. I have started recording the wild flowers in the meadow although this could get involved as the two new seeded patches mature.

May 22 (20degC. Sunny)

The first yellow flag iris opened today followed by a few others p.m. red may blossom has opened too. Between ten and fifteen damselflies hatched today, mostly 'blue tailed' but 'large red' and 'common blue' noted. Alder fly was laying its eggs on a reed (may22) and pond skaters (may22b) chased the many gnats and flies. The air was full of flying insects; their only predator seemed to be swallows. I spotted the little owl fly to and from the fallen oak so I hope they have nested successfully. Three or more 'Soprano Pipestrels' fed on the flying bugs 40 minutes after sunset.

May 23a

May 23b

May 24b

May 23c

May 23 (23degC. Sunny)
Misty start to clammy day. A few white butterflies and orange tips. Even more bugs about which pleased the swift and swallows. Moth trap contained an ermine and two brown moths plus a poplar hawk (may23c). Female Azure damsel (may23). Large Red damsel (may23a) and Blue Tailed damsel (may23b).

May 24 (25degC. Sunny)
Moth trap last night caught: White ermine, Green carpet, Coxcomb prominent (may24c), Swallow prominent (may24a), Common swift and a Cockchafer beetle (may24b). Fish were spawning from quite early so all that splash and crashing has left its mark on the marginal planting.

May 24c

May 24a

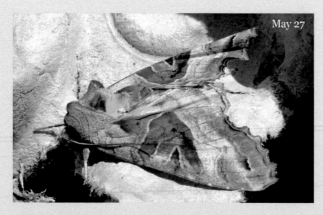
May 27

May 27d

May 26

May 25 (23degC. Sunny)
Moth trap caught a lovely eyed hawk (may25), pale tussock and a few others. Fish have carried on spawning but not as much as yesterday. Only a few orange tip butterflies.

May 26 (23degC sunny)
Only two small moths in the trap last night. Many more damsels: fifty or more on the lake, twenty or more on the ditch, some in the moat and also some large red and azure males in King's Pond. A couple of red eyed damsels (may26) showed too. Fish were basking and the grass carp were quite lively. A moorhen along with six chicks quickly hid in the brambles by the ditch no pic.

May 27 (25degC. Sunny)
Last night the moth trap caught an 'angle shades' (may27) and a tiny 'juniper pug'. First Banded demoiselle (female) (may27d) and first small copper butterfly (may27c) note blue spots on hind wing indicating that this is abb. – caerrulopunctata. While watching four squirrels chasing each other, I stumbled across a gold crest's (may27b) nest on the other side of the meadow, low in a conifer. The two parents were very busy with grub for their chicks. The millions of gnats that hatched today were hunted after dark by a number of pipestrels and daubentons bats.

May 27c

May 27b

May 25

May 28

May 29

May 30b

May 30a

May 28 (25degC. Sunny)

About a hundred damsels around the lake and several more in ditch and moat. The grey partridge seems to have lost its mate; I hope it has a nest somewhere. Goldcrest chicks you could sit two on a 2p coin. Greater spotted woodpecker has chicks in the top of the poplars and they are now fed from the 'front door'. Pool house blue tits should fly soon as should those near the feeders. I have found two more blue tits nests high in oak trees which appear to have young too. No sign of the wagtails. A few more lilies open, 'Berlin tiger' iris (may28) is in bloom and hayfield is nearly in seed. About 18.30 hrs the temperature dropped from 25 to 21 and we had a heavy shower. Clouds soon filled the sky.

May 29 (15degC. Overcast)

Cooler day with sun shining after 18.00 hrs. Small dark caterpillars feeding on unidentified plant in the meadow (may29). Two cuckoos calling together briefly. Little owls showed, they are quite brown at the moment, far from their grey winter plumage. I have set up nature-cam to try to resolve where their nest is. Many more lilies out and several more iris too.

May 30 (23degC. Sunny)

An overnight shower laid the dust but soon dried. Bad news: the goldcrest's nest has been raided possibly magpie to blame. On the up side, first brown argus butterfly and two chasers: broad bodied (may30) and four spotted. Grey partridge were together for a while and greater spotted woodpecker chicks are nearly ready to fledge (may30a). Large masses of tadpoles are circulating and their back legs are now visible. First bee orchid (may30b) in flower and more showing buds. Temperature dropped to 18degC leading to a shower.

May 30

May 31 (18degC. Cloudy)
A bit drizzly today. A Shelduck flew up from the ditch and the welcome sight of a mistle thrush (may31) with a beak full of worms confirmed they are still resident. It was raining when I saw a moorhen with EIGHT little chicks so no snapshot yet. I spotted a small 'Yellow tail' moth caterpillar at the lakeside on a blade of grass. Little owls called out after dark – although the sky was bright at 22.15 hrs.

May 31

June

Jun 1

Jun 1a

Jun 1b

Jun 01 (15degC. Overcast. SR 04.52hrs - SS 21.05hrs)

My red iris has bloomed this year and what a cracker it is! Here is the red, white and blue in honour of the Queen's Jubilee (jun1,1a,1b). The cuckoo came within sight for a while and the grey partridge seem separated. Several female long horn micro moths are evident along with click beetles and a resting damsel which moved around a stalk as I tried to get a better look.

Jun 02 (12degC. Overcast)

Tadpoles have recognisable back legs now and move around in big black masses. I found the moorhen's nest which is home to the eight chicks. Hens have started laying again but only one a day at the moment. A lovely grey partridge posed for me (jun2).

Jun 2

Jun 3

Jun 4

Jun 4b

Jun 03 (10degC. Rain)

14mm of rain since jun-01. A pair of tiny mating fourteen-spot ladybirds (jun3) was near the reeds, fused spots variation. While fishing between showers, the barn owl flew over my head. I felt sorry for it trying to find food as the long wet grass must make things difficult and apparently their feathers are not water proof because of their 'design' for silent flight.

Jun 04 (12degC. Changeable)

8degC last night and 9degC at sunset. Barn owl still hunting regularly. Woodpeckers and blue tits have fledged. Lots of pond life in the ditch: water fleas and this strange larva (jun4) of a diving beetle – Acilius sulcatus. My large 'black' iris is now in bloom (jun4b).

Jun 05 (14degC. Overcast)

Another cold night and full moon looked lovely; as it rose it was red. I spotted a tiny cricket (jun5a). Also a tiny 'marsh marigold moth' (jun5b).

Jun 5a

Jun 5b

Jun 7

Jun 8

Jun 9

Jun 10

Jun 6

Jun 06 (15degC. Rain/sun)
Full moon looked good last night but unable to see Venus pass in front of the sun this morning. I think the goldfinches have fledged, although I never did find the exact nest site. I estimate that there are at least four thousand tadpoles. Most of these have their back legs and changing body shape. A pair of harlequin ladybirds where mating on a hornbeam trunk (jun6)

Jun 07 (14degC rain)
Fine start with high winds forecast for later. Hens are laying an egg a day or more after a long spell of nothing since their broodiness. Pond lilies are looking good and plentiful but the rain could ruin them (jun7).

Jun 08 (12degC. Gales/Rain)
23mm of rain in the past three days. The 'blonde' hedgehog was out foraging in daylight (jun8).

Jun 09 (16degC. Fine)
Both barn owls were hunting in the afternoon and carried about five voles back to their nest in one hour. Wild roses are a picture (jun9).

Jun 10 (16degC. Fine)
When the sun shone it was very warm, but cloudy in the afternoon. A hairy caterpillar similar to that found a few days ago was on a blade of grass (jun10). First common blue damsel.

Jun 11 (12degC. Dreary)
Large hedgehog in the rabbit trap was please to be released this morning poor thing. A red eyed damsel lay on the grass, waterlogged. I moved him to a safer place (jun11). A few poppies were revealed after the removal of more dock plants on 'oak hill'.

Jun 11

Jun 12a

Jun 12b

Jun 13a

Jun 12 (11degC. Fine)
Barn owl man came to ring the chicks but found they were too inaccessible. He did take a picture (jun12c) though revealing at least two chicks about 30 days old. I found a grey partridge nest with seventeen eggs (jun12a) which looked abandoned; funny I hadn't seen the adults for a few days. Today I caught two small tench at 170mm long (jun12b), one male one female, so that rounded the day off nicely.

Jun 13 (15degC. Fine)
6degC. over night. A young blue tit hit the window and unfortunately died as a result. Lots of scorpion flies (jun13a) around and several blue tailed damsels but not much else. Lots of tiny amber snails and the bee orchids are in full swing, twelve in the meadow. I also spotted a beautiful 2mm long nettle weevil (jun13b): Phyllobius pomaceus

(There were two; this is the 'lesser of two weevils').

Jun 13b

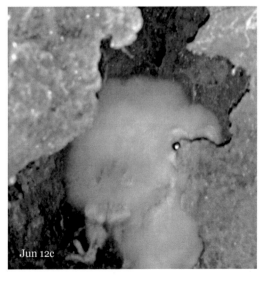

Jun 12c

Jun 14b

Jun 14

Jun 14 (16degC. Fine)

It seems to be 'bug week'; a female Privet Sawfly (Macrophya punctumalbum) (jun14) caught my eye while surveying the damsel flies. Well in excess of a hundred damsels, mostly azure, but some red eyed and blue tailed. Large red and one common blue noted. One male and one female broad bodied chaser 'chased' around and a swift swooped over the lake for a drink (jun14b). Water in King's Pond is dark and a scum over could be pollen build up. I did see a linked pair of large red damsels and a few azures though.

Jun 15 (16degC. Heavy showers)

Moles have reared their heads again and avoiding the traps. Roses are looking well (jun15) considering the gales overnight and this morning. I saw a blue bordered carpet moth but no chance of a photo.

Jun 16 (16degC. Windy/Cloudy)

Picture for today is of the lovely tiny 'scarlet pimpernel' (jun16) plant which resembles red chickweed.

Jun 16

Jun 15

Jun 18

Jun 19

Jun 19c

Jun 19b

Jun 17 (16degC. Fine)
Hundreds of frog and toadlets (jun17) are migrating from the water, only about a week or so ago when I last saw them swimming about with back legs. No butterflies still despite fine weather.

Jun 18 (17degC. Sunny intervals)
Hay field is really long now but mostly knocked flat by wind and rain. A strange caterpillar was on the herb garden wall (jun18) possibly red underwing moth.

Jun 19 (19degC. Sunny)
Fish have spawned again early this morning and possibly yesterday morning, as there were several carp feeding in the likely spawning places. Photographer heaven today; barn owl hunted early a.m. (jun19c). I found three cinnabar moths (jun19) on meadow grass near the lake, got a nice snapshot of a tiny beetle called a common malachite beetle - Malachius bipustulatus (jun19b) first four-spotted chaser, emperor dragonfly, male banded demoiselle, red admiral, common blue, meadow brown and small copper butterflies. A female broad bodied chaser showed too. This made it difficult to show photos of all these species today.

Jun 20a

Jun 21

Jun 20 (21degC. Sunny)
Fish spawning again or should I say 'still'? I found a female Poplar hawk moth (jun20a) in the long grass so I moved her to a tree trunk for safety. Dragonflies are few, female broad bodied chaser noted (jun20).

Jun 21 (18degC. Rain)
I am awaiting verification of my sighting of a 'variable damsel'. This would represent species number eighteen! Leaving the Mullion 'weed' in my garden paid off as I suspected it would attract a mullion moth. At least two caterpillars (jun21) can be seen, at only 3cm long, they will grow to 5cm.

Jun 22 (16degC. Wet & Windy)
Not much to report today as it is dull and windy. I did however find a male wood boring beetle - oedemere nobilis (jun22) (iridescent green, not so 'boring').

Jun 23 (15degC. Windy)
Very windy again with sunny intervals. The moles are at it again. Fewer young moorhens. Adult green shield bug (jun23).

Jun 23

Jun 22

Jun 24

Jun 26

Jun 25

Jun 27

Jun 24 (16degC. Wet n windy)
33mm of rain since 17th June. Just like April: rain and sunshine. Damsels on the wing as soon as the sun came out. My 'black' hollyhock is 2 metres tall and lots of buds. Stinking iris (jun24) are in bloom and roses are bloomin' lovely.

Jun 25 (18degC. Cloudy then Shine)
A major find today; a pair of Hornet clearwing moths (jun25). They are spectacular in their likeness to Hornets in markings and size. Many young birds are feeding for themselves now and still lots of tiny frogs and toads lurking in the edges of the lawn.

Jun 26b

Jun 26 (21degC. Muggy)
Figwort sawfly (jun26) caught my eye this afternoon. Beside the lake a huge horse-fly know as dark giant horse fly - Tabanus sudeticus about 40mm long, possibly freshly emerged (jun26b).

Jun 27 (21degC. Sunny)
Both barn owls hunted successfully late afternoon, at one point the male brought a vole to the nest as the female was feeding her vole to the chicks and after a little shrieking, she came and took the vole from him and into the nest, fascinating. Lots of young moorhens about (jun27).

Jun 29b

Jun 28

Jun 29a

Jun 30

Jun 28b

Jun 28 (24degC. Sunny/Stormy)
A lone four spotted chaser dragonfly mixed with a good number of azure damsels and an increasing number of common blue damsels. An emperor (jun28) showed again too. Notably several Harlequin ladybirds and their larva (jun28b). A few poppies are blooming, some that I had forgotten they were there. A couple of pretty flowers near the Gunnera behind the ditch are from some seeds I scattered in the spring. Lilies are in full swing although the yellow ones only showed one flower so far.

Jun 29 (20degC. Windy and fine)
Several meadow browns (jun29a) on the meadow (where else) and a sole male common blue (jun29b). The ditch is drying out but the moat has a good level at the moment.

Jun 30 (18degC, Fine)
A fragrance fills the air from the rose garden (jun30) and Mock range and Oleaster blossoms. Quite windy so the trees were being stretched again.

July

Jul 01 (17degC. Muggy and windy. SR 04.50hrs – SS 21.14hrs)

Another yellow lily in flower but they don't seem very yellow. Thalia Delbata should be sprouting buds soon. Yellow fringe lily (jul1) is in full swing and will need stemming soon.

Jul 02 (17degC. Showers)

Welcome rain but only enough to irritate me. Hay making is on hold till the forecast is good for three or four days. Despite lack of sunshine, meadow browns and ringlets on the wing. Roses are still very good (jul2) and honeysuckle is lovely (jul2b).

Jul 03 (17degC. Rain)

Mistle thrush (jul3) caught my eye as it pestered a jay which looked like it was 'anting' (putting ants under its feathers to rid parasites by way of the formic acid they give off in defence). Green woodpeckers are often about but very shy.

Jul 3

Jul 2a

Jul 2b

Jul 4a

Jul 4

Jul 4b

Jul 5b

Jun 04 (21degC. Showers/sun)
Very humid day ten or more butterflies:
meadow brown, ringlet, speckled wood,
red admiral, gate keeper and one common
blue. Magpie moth and lacewings (jul4a)
along with several harlequin ladybird
larvae. Also, a robber fly caught a crane
fly and devoured it (jul4). A young
spotted woodpecker found an ant's nest
and was happily licking them up. A
dense web was being guarded by Mrs
Nursery Web spider (jul4b).
Jul 05 (24degC. Humid)
A few carp were spawning this morning.
Poppies 'Maltese Cross' are looking
great (jul5). First hornet of this year
landed on the privet flowers and a male
broad bodied chaser dragonfly flew past.
Nice to see Amphibious bistort (jul5b)
in flower, I wait to see if the grass carp
eats it all this year. A small trace of
oxygenating weed so fingers crossed it
also survi

Jul 5

Jul 06 (18degC. Rain/Sunny)
A few large skippers about in the afternoon (jul6), along with several meadow browns. (female jul6a). More Ringlets now and a solitary red admiral. What I thought was a baby rabbit was caught in the cage trap this morning and turned out to be a leveret.

Jul 07 (18degC. Changeable/ humid)
12mm of rain in the past few days. Speckled wood butterflies in the lane and a female southern hawker dragonfly (jul7a). In the meadow there are lots of large ant's nests and I spotted a few young Roesel's bush crickets (jul7) and knapweed, which I don't remember seeing before. Gnats are biting well.

Jul 08 17degC. Rain)
No crab apples, walnuts and not many conkers. I hope there will be hazel nuts. Overall it was a drab day. Heron was stalking the fish this morning (jul8).

Jul 9

Jul 10a

Jul 11a

Jul 10

Jul 11

Jul 09 (17degC. Fine)
Several butterflies, mostly meadow browns but also a red admiral and some ringlets and small skippers (jul9). Again I tried to establish some oxygenator weed in the lake, this time ring-fencing it. I checked out King's Pond, turbid but most plants are growing, notably the pickerel weed.

Jul 10 (17degC. Changeable)
Last night I rescued a mouse (jul10a) from Ziggy, it looked in good condition but although it seemed to be a bit slow, it still out manoeuvred Ziggy for a while. I found another hornet clearwing moth near the poplars. The meadow-mats are very pretty now (jul10). One male gatekeeper (jul10b) appeared amongst several butterflies on the wing.

Jul 11 (17degC. Rain/Sun)
I found another hornet moth and discovered the larvae exit holes and an empty pupa at the base of the poplars. A few butterflies took to the wing when the sun shone and a male banded demoiselle (jul11) showed amongst a few freshly emerged damsels. Fabulous longhorn beetle (Strangalia maculata) in the meadow (jul11a).

Jul 10b

Jul 12

Jul 12 (16degC. Sun/Rain)

After a short visit to Pakenham woods to look for silver washed fritillary butterflies, I spotted this year's first purple hairstreak but unable to photograph. Both barn owls were sitting in the 'owl oak' keeping an eye on me. I then looked for more hornet moths and found some tiny snails, plaited door snails (jul12) and raced to cut the grass before it rained.

Jul 13 (16degC. Overcast)

Last night 12mm of rain fell so it was soggy this morning. Green woodpeckers are finding ants nests and feeding most of the day. Sea holly (jul13) is thriving at the moment. Small droppings similar to mouse poo has appeared on the step of the pool house door. I suspect that bats are roosting under the fascia board, so I have setup the nature-cam tonight.

Jul 14 (15degC Rain/sun)

Lots of pond skaters, mostly smaller ones. When the sun did shine in the afternoon, gatekeeper, ringlet, meadow brown and small skippers showed in numbers. A short fishing session resulted in a only a few fish but one common carp at 8 lb. The Thalia (jul14) is the best it has ever been with it's great stalks, and flowers now opening.

Jul 15 (17degC. Fair)

Breezy and cool. Barn owl busy hunting, I would imagine the two chicks are feathered and require lots of food. A few harlequin ladybirds and a fourteen spot ladybird larvae (jul15) about. Later, barn owls took at least three voles & mice to their nest within twenty minutes! Good to know.

Jul 13

Jul 15

Jul 14

Jul 16

Jul 17

Jul 18

Jul 19

Jul 16 (15degC. Rain)

First brown hawker flew past when I was in the meadow and later, a lovely leveret ran towards me and ran away when it saw me. A short while later, a roe deer doe with a fawn wasn't sure weather to stay or run, they decided to run. Black hollyhocks in bloom (jul16).

Jul 17 (20degC. Sun/Muggy/rain)

Good count of butterflies in the sun: meadow brown, ringlet, gatekeeper, small and large skippers, one purple hairstreak, one red admiral and one large white. A solitary female banded demoiselle gave me the slip so no photo. Two barn owls at the nest passed a vole between them but I couldn't be sure if one was a 'chick' although it did seem to stumble about the branches.

Jul 18 (17degC. Showers)

Two barn owls stumbling around near their nest I feel are this years youngsters. (jul17). They are beautiful, I got to within a few feet of them preening and playing. There are now two shrews which Ziggy brought home, maybe pigmy or water shrew barely 5cm long excluding tail. Yet another family of moorhens! (jul18).

Jul 19 (16degC. Rain)

A few butterflies and damsels out between showers and Barn owls busy. Cinnabar moth caterpillars have showed on the ragwort (jul19).

Jul 21

Jul 21b

Jul 20

Jul 20 (15degC. Showers)

After starting hay cutting yesterday, James finished off this morning. A couple of young green woodpeckers were calling for their parents in the garden this morning, before it rained. 16mm of rain since 13th July. Baby moorhen (jul20).

Jul 21 (18degC. Sunny)

Very warm in the sun which brought out lots of damsels and butterflies. A small but eye-catching, gooseberry sawfly (jul21) eventually posed for a photo. Ten or more swifts dive bombed the lake at great speed, skimming the surface. As yet unidentified moth (jul21b) was the only one in the trap this morning.

Jul 22 (21degC. Sunny)

First sighting of common darters (jul22). Large white and lots of skippers again. Scarce footman in the moth trap.

Jul 22

Jul 24c

Jul 24a

Jul 24b

Jul 24

Jul 23 (27degC. Sunny)
Brown hawker and first mating pair of
Black tailed skimmers (jul23) came out
in the hot sun while young Barn owl
slept in the shade (jul23b). A pair of
banded demoiselles showed too.

Jul 24 (27degC. Sunny)
Sixty or so moths in the trap, including
one drinker moth (jul24b). Several
banded demoiselles out today, one female
which was a lovely colour (jul24a). Hay
bailing was in full swing (jul24c) as the
sun shone from a cloudless sky. I finally
got round to removing some of the fringe
lilies (jul24).

Jul 23

Jul 23b

Jul 25

Jul 27

Jul 25 (29degC. Sunny)
Another drinker moth in the trap along with a few tiny interesting micro-moths. I found a pair of ruddy darter (jul25) dragonflies near the ditch, good news as the Moat colony perished in the drought last year.

Jul 26 (26degC. Sunny)
Misty start to another hot and humid day. Moth trap revealed drinker, oak eggar, pine hawk (jul26Right), privet hawk (jul26Left), swallow prominent and a thorn. When I shut the hens in, I stumbled upon a large emerald moth.

Jul 27 (22degC. Sunny)
A Brown Hawker female gave me the slip so no photo, but confirmation of essex skippers (jul27) and first seen six spot burnet moth (jul27a). First holly blue butterfly of the year too. I have now recorded eighty different moths and twenty one different butterflies since 'records began'. A pair of hedgehogs were out tonight, looked like they were courting??

Jul 28 (19degC. Sunny)
Cooler morning, moles are on the move again. Pollarded willows are bushy (jul28) and grass growing despite no rain. I saw the six spot burnet again and two red admirals. A strange accumulation of saw flies on a grass stem and I notice yet another family of moorhens.

Jul 2

Jul 26

Jul 28

Jul 30

Jul 29

Jul 31a

Jul 29 (17degC. Fine/Storm)
I pumped some water from the lake to save the ditch drying out and maybe save some newts and ruddy darters. It only rained twice: once when I rolled out the pump hose and once when I checked the mole traps. I still haven't found where the black and white hen (Wyandotte bantam?) is laying her eggs. I also spotted a rather striking looking hover fly (eupeodes nitens) (jul29).

Jul 30 (16degC. Sunny/showers)
A commotion near the paddocks turned out to be birds mobbing a red kite (jul30). It looked like a juvenile but look how it compares in size to the crow! I am trying to i.d. a tiny caterpillar I found on grass.

Jul 31 (14degC. Showers)
1.5mm rain yesterday. (jul31). I rescued a Crested newt (jul31a) from the entrance to a wasp nest that I had put wasp powder in. I hope it wasn't affected by it, it was drowsy but that is normal out of water. Temperature rose to 18degC by evening but very overcast by then.

August

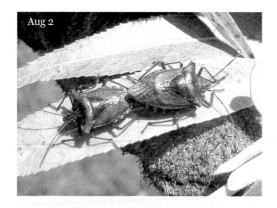

Aug 01 (19degC. Fine)
1.5mm rain since last reading. Fish are ravenous still and seem healthy despite a recent dead carp which I retrieved from the island, maybe heron issue. A kestrel was leisurely hunting as the sun was getting low (aug1).

Aug 02 (19degC, Muggy)
Moth trap caught a pale prominent (aug2a) and an early thorn not much else. 4.5mm of rain today, breezy with some sun. A pair of red legged shield bugs (aug2) was mating in a weeping willow. Moles are becoming a nuisance again, now it has rained I will need to reset the traps.

Aug 03 (18degC. Muggy)
More different flowers from the 'meadow mat' (aug3). Several essex and small skippers in the meadow and a few meadow browns. The ground is hard and dry and the ditch is almost dry again. 0.5 mm of rain is less than most of East Anglia.

Aug 04 (20degC. Showers)
Blackbirds (aug4) are eating the Rowan berries already so I guess they must be ripe early. Full moon last night maybe that had an effect on the lack of any moths in the trap. Thunderstorms passed on either side again giving us a measly few drops of rain.

Aug 5

Aug 6

Aug 8

Aug 05 (18degC. Showers)

5.5mm of rain mostly in one shower and thunder storms nearby. Still lots of hover flies about (aug5).

Aug 06 (18degC. Humid/showers)

Only a few moths in the trap this morning, notably one was a herald (au6). Ditch is almost dry now but King's Pond and the moat are still OK. Very few butterflies and a couple of damsels showed and little owls called out. I did see a small butterfly high in the trees which was either holly blue or purple hairstreak.

Aug 07 (17degC. Showers)

1.5mm of rain today. Not much to report except that the hay fields are getting very green already, and everywhere looks quite lush (aug7).

Aug 08 (18degC. Fine)

Hundreds of new pond skaters. A poor little hedgehog in the garden had flies around it and they had laid eggs near one eye, it seemed well enough but I did try to clear some of the eggs. Blackbirds still raiding the rowan berries. A Willow warbler with its irritating 'tweet' sunbathed and preened (aug8).

Aug 7

Aug 9b

Aug 9

Aug 10b

Aug 09 (22degC. Sunny)
A few interesting moths in the trap: ruby tiger (aug9b) copper underwing and lesser broad bordered yellow underwing. Purple hairstreak (aug9) showed briefly but high in the oak tree. While clearing weeds from 'Oak Hill' I saw a number of small toads and frogs. When I was watching the swallows sitting on the TV Ariel, a sparrow hawk swooped down and chased one of them. Last night I had fun watching the bats feed over the lake before it got too dark.

Aug 10 (22degC. Sunny)
I managed to photograph the illusive brown hawker (aug10) which is laying eggs in the margins normally out of clear view. A few moths in the trap this morning including a white satin moth (aug10b).

Aug 10

Aug 11

Aug 11b

Aug 11a

Aug 11 (21degC. Sunny)

I thought I saw a red squirrel in the top of a large Holly tree today but it turned out to be a stoat! It was higher than the overhead telephone cables and running through the branches, I didn't see it come down. At least four male banded damsels and one female. I spotted over four Holly Blues (aug11b), red admiral (aug11), comma, and an elusive peacock (aug11c). Harvestman (leiobunum rotundum) (aug11a) also noted. While walking in Oak Road I glimpsed a male humming bird hawk moth but no photo opportunity.

Aug 11c

Aug 12

Aug 13

Aug 14

Aug 14b

Aug 12 (23degC. Sunny)
A pair of migrant hawkers patrolled the meadow (female aug12) while a small number of browns and a few skippers and a brown argus fed. There appears to be lots of hawthorn berries this year but zero crab apples, there are several plums and sloes swelling already.

Aug 13 (22DegC.fine/shower)
A green woodpecker found an ant's nest near the bird feeders (aug13). Still several male banded damsels plus one female. When I checked the mole traps, a little owl flew from a Holm oak and later, two barn owls flew from the owl oak when I was on rabbit patrol. In addition to the Crab apple trees dropping their leaves, an established thorn tree looks like it is dying. The same fate as a Beech and a Lime recently.

Aug 14 (22degC. Showers/Sun)
A pair of mating red tailed bumble bees looked a little uncomfortable as they hung on to a tree trunk (aug14) note the tics attached to the queen. One small copper butterfly (aug14b) showed this afternoon.

Aug 15

Aug 15a

Aug 15 (22degC. Fine/Drizzle)
Magpies raided the fish food (aug15a). Lots of dark bush crickets (aug15b) on the meadow and grasshoppers too (aug15).
Aug 16 (33DegC. Fine)
Several green finch and chaffinch gathering to feed. Swallows are still about but no sign of any swifts now or martins. Caught a few moths, notably a pretty micro moth and a dingy footman (aug16).

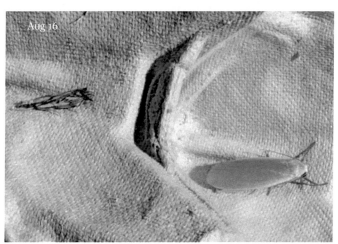

Aug 16

Aug 15b

Aug 17b.

Aug 17c

Aug 17

Aug 18

Aug 19

Aug 17 (26degC. Sunny & windy)
A few more holly blues and by chance spotted a female dingy footman moth (ab. - stramineola) (aug17b). A song thrush is making regular visits across the lake with snails from the garden which is good news on both fronts. Yellow-tail moth (aug17) and a few micros this morning. Had a surprise as a Lesser Stag Beetle (aug17c) dropped to the floor when I checked the hens.

Aug 18 (31.4degC. Sunny)
It is 20.30 hrs and it is still 26degC. I found two male common blue butterflies (male aug18) in the meadow which was a nice surprise. Also a brown argus, small copper and a pair of migrant hawkers showed. Later on a southern hawker flew by. Lots of swallows swirling about and Mrs Song thrush is still busy transporting snails. The fish did some sun bathing in the afternoon, I counted eighteen decent carp over 4 lb in addition to those feeding at the bench.

Aug 19 (29degC. Sunny/Stormy)
Very humid. Lots of moths in the trap this morning tried a new position near the other end of the pool house. Quite an assortment, including a forest bug (aug19) and loads of leaf beetles. Couldn't find any Hairstreaks today but I did see a variety of butterflies in small numbers including a pair of speckled wood. A rumble of thunder but only a few spots of rain.

Aug 20 (26degC. Sunny)
First capture of a 'maiden's blush', a small and dainty moth (aug20). No damsels today and not many butterflies either. Nights are drawing in noticeably now.

Aug 21 (22degC. Sunny)
Cooler day but humid, cloudy at times but no sign of needed rain. A huge Leopard Slug was licking the cat's bowl clean this morning (aug21).

Aug 22 (21degC. Fine/cloudy)
Cool night at about 15degC. Still dry bar a light shower in the afternoon. A few butterflies on the meadow when the sun shone, namely brown argus (aug22a), common blue, small copper, small skipper, Essex skipper and gatekeepers. One female gatekeeper was a bit tatty but was an aberration 'excessa' (aug22b), as the photo shows clearly the extra spots and double 'pupils' in the fore wing spot.

Aug 23

Aug 23b

Aug 23 (21degC. Fine)
Last night I watched the Daubenton's and Pipistrelle bats flying about; there was a lot of flying insects for them. More speckled woods and small coppers (aug23b), and other odds. I spotted one of the Thrush chicks flying clumsily into brambles. Several strange acorn galls possibly knopper galls (aug23) on the old oak in the garden. Ditch side is maturing (aug23c).

Aug 24 (20egC. Fine)
More than a dozen Speckled Woods amongst the butterfly list today. Resting dragonflies were order of the day and I was very lucky to photograph the southern hawker (aug24c) close up, no such luck for the pair of migrant hawkers (male aug24b) which rested high in a tree. A sexton beetle (aug24a) was hiding in the moth trap. This beetle is the size of a thumbnail and is one of a few UK burying beetles.

Aug 24a

Aug 24b

Aug 23c

Aug 24c

Aug 25

Aug 26

Aug 27

Aug 25 (20degC. Rain)
9mm of rain today and some storms about. Swallows are feeding their fledglings on the TV mast (aug25). At night a tawny owl hooted, very dark and very wet out there.

Aug 26 (20degC. Fine)
Today I saw at least four migrant hawkers and a possible emperor. Two more trees are now confirmed dead but we will see if there is actually any life left in the spring. A small, pale earwig sat on a tree protector (aug26).

Aug 27 (19degC. Showers)
A good deal of distress calls near the lake turned out to be a weasel killing a moorhen; it soon dragged the carcass off to cover. Nearby, I spotted a hawthorn shield bug (aug27).

Aug 28a

Aug 28b

Aug 28c

Aug 28 (20degC. Fine)

Removed all signs of the Fringe lily today while the weather was fine and water level down, it remains to be seen how quickly it returns. First capture of a mother of pearl moth (aug28a) one or two about in the vicinity of the lane. Migrant hawkers, common darters and a couple of blue tailed damsels showed in the sunny intervals. At least three red admirals fed on the pile of windfall apples that I moved to near the he house. Good news too: I found a small heath butterfly (aug28b), a Green Farm first. Caught a glimpse of a buzzard overhead later on (aug28c). I spotted a tatty comma on the budlea and also a small tortoiseshell.

Aug 29 (20degC. Windy)

First summer photo of a small tortoiseshell (aug29b) and now another handsome comma (aug29). Temperature dropped to 15degC p.m. and rain set in.

Aug 29

29b

Aug 30

Aug 31

Aug 30 (15degC. Rain)
Full moon tonight, it was bright and quite full last night too. 5mm of rain in the last 24 hours. I am investigating whether there is more than one type of pond skater as Suffolk Biodiversity are interested in sightings of 'Aquarius paludum' which I have reported that we have here. Finally found a nicely marked male migrant hawker amongst several on the wing today, so I cheated and replaced august 24th's image with the one taken today. Sloes and blackberries (aug30) are coming on and hawthorn berries are on the turn.

Aug 31 (18degC. Fine)
Spotted a mid instar of a dock bug - Coreus marginatus (aug31). A few red admirals about and I spotted a brown argus and one male common blue. Still a few migrant hawkers when the sun shines. The fish are feeding well and some look like they have gained weight again. Full moon tonight though it is cloudy. There goes August.

September

Sep 1

Sep 1a

Sep 01 (18degC. Fine SR 06.10 – SS 19.48)

Adrian Chalkley at Suffolk Naturalists's Society has confirmed that the pond skaters on the lake are 'Aquarius paludum'. This is only the second recorded sighting of them in Suffolk. While cutting the grass (for how long now?) I spied a long winged conehead (sep1a) and as I photographed that, I saw a black ichneumon wasp (sep1) which apparently is difficult to identify accurately as there are over three thousand species in the UK! Today it was nice to see the young song thrushes (sep1b) that have survived.

Sep 02 (19degC. Cloudy)

Moth trap revealed a pretty micro moth and a light emerald (sep2). The herons lifted a small carp out of the water and left it to die. Lots of crickets in the meadow as usual this time of the year and also a lot of crane flies hatching out, again usual for the end of summer.

Sep 1b

Sep 2

Sep 3   Sep 4b

Sep 3a   Sep 3b

Sep 03 (20degC. Sunny)

After a very misty night, this morning, the moth trap revealed only a few moths but I found a pair of red underwings (sep3a, b) on the pool house, they are quite big with a wing span of about 70mm. While stalking a female common blue, I stumbled on to a mirid bug *corizus hyoscyami* (sep3) a striking small fellow. Swallows still feeding and resting on the TV mast. Lots of red admirals were feeding on the windfall apples; I counted seven and a few speckled woods.

Sep 04 (22degC. Fine)

Sunny morning but cloudy p.m. Three male banded demoiselles have appeared but no females in sight. green shield beetle, dark bush crickets and meadow grasshoppers showed and I counted ten red admirals under the apple trees. When I was photographing a green shield bug (sep4c) I spotted a speckled bush cricket (sep4). On the walk back I saw this pesky squirrel (sep4b) probably with a stolen hazel nut.

Sep 4

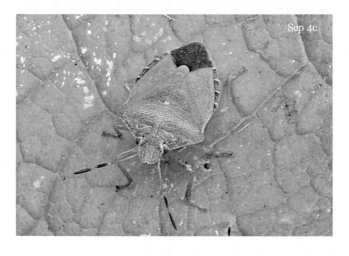

Sep 4c

Sep 5

Sep 5b

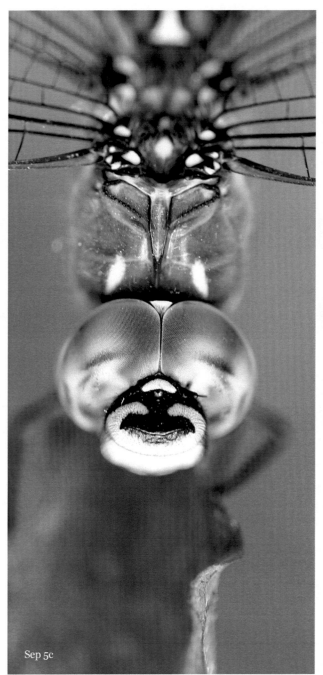

Sep 5c

Sep 05 (19degC. Sunny)
Seemed warmer than 19 deg. And quite breezy. Four herons flew up this morning. A male migrant hawker landed right in front of me today and luckily, camera in hand, I took some good close-ups (sep5c). The female brown argus butterfly spotted yesterday has been identified as a rare aberration making it similar to a northern brown argus due to white spots on the upper side of its wings (sep5). Clematis on the flint wall is in bloom again (sep5b) and a possible i.d. on the trees in the cover belt is wild Medlar. At dusk about thirty geese flew over but none of them decided to land.

Sep 06 (19degC. Fine)
Cool damp night. I have been away all day so got back Just in time to shut the chickens in and feed the fish (and Ziggy) sun was very low but red lilies are still looking good (sep6).

Sep 6

Sep 7

Sep 8

Sep 9

Sep 9b

Sep 07 (22degC. Sunny)
Not a cloud in the sky after a cool dewy morning. A weasel nipped between the flower border and the meadow but no chance of a photo. Hips and haws are getting ripe (sep7). Darn partridges are about again raiding the hens' food etc.

Sep 08 (26degC. Sunny)
Hedgehog out feeding last night and moth trap revealed a few moths including a centre barred sallow (sep8). A couple of blue tailed damsels showed along with a female brown hawker, mating pair of migrant hawkers and the usual common darters, some mating. Hopefully the lone female banded demoiselle will find one of the males that I saw earlier.

Sep 09 (27degC. Sunny)
Grass is getting a bit brown now as we have no rain for a while. I found a toadstool in the cover belt which could be a 'scaly earthball' (sep9). Heron loitering again. While fishing just before dusk, a tiny short tailed vole popped out for a meal, just inches away from my foot (sep9b). I also caught the large Tench and a lovely smaller one (sep9c), a rare catch.

Sep 9c

Sep 10

Sep 10b

Sep 11

Sep 10 (21degC. Sunny)
Blackberries are ripening well in some places (sep10). A small hedgehog was feeding in daylight poor thing, note to self: put some food out for it. Squirrels have found the hazel nuts on the other side of the lake now there are none. The grape vine is very full now (sep10b).

Sep 11 (17degC. Sunny)
Squirrels have polished off the remaining hazelnuts. Still a few red admirals and a pair of lovely commas too. I heard a bird singing a very pretty song but I couldn't see it, I think it was a whitethroat. Photo of the day is a green shield bug fifth instar (sep11). In the morning a young heron landed clumsily on the top of a Eucalyptus tree (sep11b).

Sep 12

Sep 13

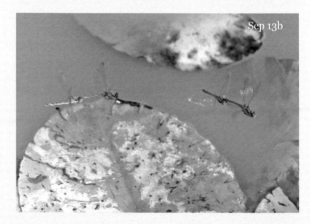
Sep 14

Sep 13b

Sep 12 (15degC. Showers)
Fine day till late afternoon. Three swallows swooped about in the rain; I guess they will be the last this year. Hedgerows are becoming red with haw berries and leaves are starting to blow into corners. A hundred or so crows squawked in one mass about 15.00 hrs. (sep12). 8mm of rain at dusk.

Sep 13 (17degC. Fine)
Heavy dew stayed most of the day and it became quite windy. Several common darters coupled (sep13b) and a lone brown hawker. A few red admirals and commas on the wing. Days are much shorter now so not long to go to the Equinox. An unusual toadstool (sep13) has appeared on an Elm stump which I have yet to identify (dryads saddle, bracket fungi. Polyporus squamosus).

Sep 14 (17degC. Windy/cloudy)
One Swallow still here, battling the gusts of wind. migrant hawker, brown hawker and common darter showed along with red admiral, comma and large white. While strimming the lakeside I spotted a knotgrass moth caterpillar (sep14a) and later, a green lacewing (sep14). I found the small hedgehog dead by the moat, no apparent cause of death.

Sep 14a

Sep 15

Sep 15a

Sep 16

Sep 17

Sep 15 (20degC. Sunny)
Managed a couple of hours fishing but still only tiddlers. Two male brown hawkers and two male migrant hawkers eluded photo capture of any quality (sep15) and one swallow passed by. I heard signs that the young song thrushes are still well, but no sign of the barn owls for a while. Lots of common hawkers still making the most of the fine weather (sep15a).

Sep 16 (18degC. Fine/windy)
Still the odd swallow about and a wren often buzzing around the reeds. A short float fishing session before dusk resulted in several two pounders and a cracking 8 lb common. When I eventually landed it after five to ten minutes, a four pound mirror jumped in the net with it! (sep16).

Sep 17 (19degC. Sunny)
A few dragonflies (sep17) and a lone damsel. A crab apple tree that seemed to be dying has new leaves and since the dropping of a few apples it now has some blossom!

Sep 18

Sep 21

Sep 19

Sep 20

Sep 18 (16degC. Sun/wind + shower)
Squirrels are appearing in unlikely places, possible burying nuts. Brown hawker and migrant hawker still about and a few red admirals. Some yew hedges have lots of berries (sep18).

Sep 19 (15degC. Fine)
Sunny and breezy again with dark clouds building as I write this note. In the afternoon, I came across a box bug with a late instar box bug (sep19). The limes in the avenue are colouring up and some leaves are falling, the poplars too. I was only just thinking that I hadn't seen the barn owl and hey presto, I saw him hunting at sunset. Early sunsets now about 19.15 hrs.

Sep 20 (17degC. Fine)
Two roe deer passed by and later I found evidence of them nibbling the dogwood. The kestrel was keeping local but was mobbed by crows. Reflections were pretty as sun set (sep20).

Sep 21 (15degC fine/overcast)
I had to retrieve a fish from the island which had been killed by an early heron. The well pump has been running for three days to offset the lake water level drop; a shower at dusk was welcome. I just missed a photo chance of a linked pair of migrant hawkers. Nightshade is fruiting and looks quite nice (sep21).

Sep 23

Sep 22

Sep 22 (14degC. Fine)
7mm in the rain gauge this morning. Barn owl hunting mid afternoon and southern hawker was obliging (sep22). A couple of swallows still about.

Sep 23 (11degC. Fine/rain)
Very cold last night. Chiffchaff calling like it is spring. Everything is green at the moment (sep23) but as the Equinox has passed, cooler shorter days are on the way so things will change.

Sep 24 (13degC. Rain)
17mm of rain since yesterday and more most of today, about a further 7mm. quite windy too. The donated muskovy ducks have arrived and are in the old hen house for a few days. The lovely white roses by the farmhouse door have been spoilt by the wind and rain

Sep 24

Sep 25 (15degC. Fine)

Windy again and only short spells worth trying to get a photo for today. Only thing of consequence was a final instar woundwort shield bug (sep25). Squirrels still being a nuisance.

Sep 26 (14degC. Overcast)

Light showers adding to 1mm of rain since Sep 24. A few green shield bugs sunbathed on leaves near the meadow and squirrels continued to steal conkers. A couple of swallows were still evident and a poorly hedgehog should not be out in daylight. A well moonlit night, a plume moth possibly Emmelina monodactyla landed on the window attracted by the light (sep26).

Sep 27 (14degC. Fine)

Ducks are settling in and I anticipate their release tomorrow. Lots of sawfly grubs (sep27) eating the privet and many green shield bugs too.

Sep 28 (14degC. damp/overcast)

I fed the ducks early morning and opened their door, one young one came out and walked back in and fed. Later I discover that they flew away and found their previous home! Surely the last sighting of a swallow and still a few butterflies and dragonflies. A weasel ran across the drive at speed to take cover in long grass (sep28a).

Sep 29

Sep 29 (15degC. Fine/windy) Full moon. (sep29)
A noisy day as light aircraft and several tractors roared away
constantly.
Sep 30 (15degC. Fine/windy) (sep30)
A few pond skaters about and the odd dragonfly or two. Little
owls were calling in the afternoon and evidence of fox activity.

Sep 30

October

Oct 1

Oct 1b

Oct 2

Oct 2c

Oct 2b

Oct 01 (15degC. Showers. SR – 07.00hrs SS – 18.41hrs)
A few roe deer grazed in a neighbouring field while the little owls called and flitted past. A strange fungus is growing on a fallen oak limb (oct1). Barn owl out at sunset and a huge frog (oct1b) and some newts by the flint wall including three crested newts, one quite small and the others large females.

Oct 02 (15degC. Fine/windy)
A few swallows still about, surely they will be leaving soon. Two flies coremacera marginata were mating, not very polite but I did get a photo (oct2). Still coupled pairs of common darters too. A dainty limoniid crane fly stopped for a photo (oct2b). Beautiful sunset (oct2c).

Oct 3

Oct 5

Oct 4

Oct 03 (14degC. Changeable)
A buzzard on the next field caught a bird, looked like a Jay. It was pestered to drop it by two crows. A tiny nettle tap moth - *Anthophila fabriciana* rested on a sunny flower (oct3).

Oct 04 (13degC. Fine)
'Barny' showed today and the buzzard returned with a low fly-by. A sparrowhawk swooped by the feeders but didn't catch anything. One pied wagtail tweeted on the farmhouse roof, I haven't seen any since late spring. The new Rowan tree has some pretty berries and the autumn leaves could be good too (oct4).

Oct 05 (13degC. Changeable)
17mm of rain fell overnight. A knotgrass moth caterpillar was feeding on the dogwood, possibly the same one I found earlier but now much bigger (oct5a). Could the stray cat (oct5) be Ziggy's Dad? Lots of conkers have now fallen in the gusty wind and rain. Winter sunflowers brighten up the ditch edge (oct5b).

Oct 5a

Oct 06 (13degC. Sunny)
A cute little furry caterpillar (oct6) of a muslin moth fed in the sun while SIX buzzards wheeled overhead. The air became thick with aphids (oct6a) in the afternoon.

Oct 07 (12degC. Fine)
Cool day with some sun till dusk. A strange fungus has appeared on the ditch 'stepping stones' possibly wolf's milk - lycogala terrestre, a slime mould (oct7). Misty start and a misty end (oct7b)

Oct 08 (13degC. Fine)
More various toadstools about and lots of dock Bugs (oct8b) on.... Dock leaves! Also a bronze shield bug (oct8) on privet. After sunset a pipestrelle bat zoomed around the outbuildings (oct8c).

Oct 9

Oct 9a

Oct 9b

Oct 09 (12degC. Sunny)
Little owls called loudly close by and
barn owl hunted early (16.00hrs).
The wasp nest in the lawn is still
lively (oct9b). Glistening crumble
cap toadstools are abundant (oct9).
A jay sneaked in for a meal courtesy
of the hens' food (oct9a).

Oct 10 (13degC. Sunny)
Both heron and cormorant (oct10) eyed up the fish this morning and little owl and barn owl hunted in the afternoon. Near to dusk, a few small ducks thought about landing but they saw me and flew away. I think they might have been Teal. A buzzard was chased away by four crows and the light breeze dropped to make a lovely calm sunset (oct10b).

Oct 11 (13degC. Showers)
Fine to start but breezy. I was clearing old barbed wire when, metres away, a huge branch snapped off the large oak (oct11). First sighting this year of a black slug by the lake (oct11b). Good to see that two more pied wagtails have arrived to keep the other one company.

Oct 12

Oct 13b

Oct 12 (12degC. Sunny/cloudy)
3mm of rain last night although it seemed like more. A cormorant surfaced in the shallow water of the lake this morning and left empty 'handed'. Colourful toadstools, like orange peel, littered the ground beneath the trees in the far cover belt (oct12). One solitary comma butterfly fed on brambles in the sun.

Oct 13 (13degC. Sunny)
Some cloud and turning cold at dusk (9degC). A beautiful garden spider (oct13) escaped the willow cuttings as I cleared up. More various toadstools including ink caps popping up everywhere. One red admiral was noted. Finally got around to adapting the old tawny owl nest box (oct13b) with the addition of a porch. This should, I hope, catch the interest of little owls.

Oct 13

Oct 14b

Oct 16

Oct 15

Oct 14 (11degC. Fine)
My attention was draw to the sound of three skylarks singing and chasing over the stubble field, while the first brambling (oct14c) of this winter, fed beneath the bird feeders. Later as the clouds drew in, a buzzard flew over mobbed by crows as usual. Other strange fungi on a stump (oct14b) over the pond's edge could be shaggy scale cap, but I will check in a day or two. Rain at dusk.

Oct 15 (11degC.showers)
6degC overnight and 2mm of rain. Cup fungus on elder (oct15) with a kind of lichenised fungi or maybe a kind of disco. Ink caps are maturing elsewhere. Birds are busy at the feeders but no sign of the bramblings today.

Oct 16 (13degC. Windy)
Gales made it a chilly day. Jays and woodpeckers showed and I startled a roe deer but no photo. Pretty toadstool: Little Japenese Umbrella amongst many (oct16).

Oct 14c

Oct 18a

Oct 18c

Oct 17 (13degC. Fine)
Wet start and 6mm of rain since 15th. Red oak is err, red! Photo tomorrow. Autumn colours are starting to show (oct17).

Oct 18 (14degC. Fine)
Four pied wagtails on the farm house roof this morning. Red oak (oct18a) looked better in bright sun, not much of that today. A cute fairy ring (oct18b) near the weeping willow, about 1 metre across. Another toadstool has popped up (oct18c) a yellow centred bonnet variety.

Oct 18b

Oct 17

Oct 19 (14degC. Rain)

Fine start but degraded after breakfast. Even more fungi appearing in the grass like these small toadstools possibly Galerina Mycenopsis (oct19a) and Shaggy Ink Caps (oct19b). I will take a rain gauge reading in the morning. Later, in the mild wet darkness, a large female crested newt (oct19c) was finishing off a huge worm, yum! Yum!

Oct 20

Oct 20a

Oct 20b

Oct 20 (13degC. Fine)
18mm of rain since last reading. A pair of redwings flew over while a few last coupled pairs of common darters laid their eggs. More unusual fungi: hairy curtain crust (oct20a) and unknown (oct20. I was shocked to see a solitary bat (oct20b), possibly a Leisler's bat, circling overhead; it was as big as a blackbird I would say, unusual for mid afternoon.

Oct 21 (11degC. Drizzle) 9mm of rain last night followed by a drab day. Something is creeping and tapping in the roof again, I hope it's a blue tit or at worst, a bat. Eye-catching toadstools near the bird feeders (oct21 & 21b).

Oct 21 b

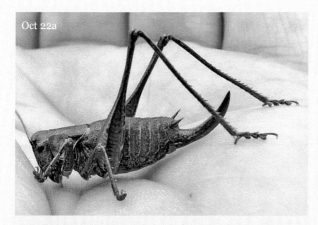

Oct 22 (13degC. Foggy)
Autumn colours (oct22c) are expanding and toadstools continue to appear including a few blue roundheads (oct22b) and clustered bonnet - mycena inclinata (oct22d). Green woodpeckers often darting about in search of food on the lawns. Some Dark Bush Crickets (oct22a) are taking refuge in the bonfire pile.

Oct 23

Oct 23b

Oct 23 (14degC. Foggy)
Overnight a small area of blackening wax caps (oct23) popped up, they will quickly turn black and decay. Seems a bit late for fifth instar Woundwort shield bugs (oct23b). Unusual small crab spider - Philodromus dispar found near the bonfire (oct23c).

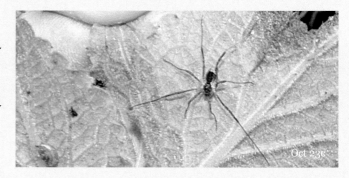

Oct 23c

Oct 24 (13degC. Misty)
Mild and damp today. Mr Heron was very keen to hang around as the fish were up in the water which is clearing gradually. I rescued a vapourer moth (oct24a) from the lake just in time I reckon. sulphur tufts (oct24) at the lake side.

Oct 25 (11degC. Overcast)
While clipping the Bay tree, I found an oak bush-cricket (oct25). Fish are looking big and fat and the water is clearing now. A few more fieldfares flew over but I haven't seen any feeding on the berries yet.

Oct 26b

Oct 26

Oct 28

Oct 26 (10degC. Cloudy)
Moles are spreading from the fields again, making hills in the lawns. The Parrotia tree is pretty as it changes from green to red (oct26). Masses of toadstools appeared from mulched chippings under the trees (oct26b).

Oct 27 (6degC. Rain/Hail)
Morning gale blew a dead elm over and a breeze all day made it very cold. New Larch, Irish Yew, Catalpa and Dawn Redwood 'gold rush' (oct27) trees planted today between showers.

Oct 28 (7degC. Overcast)
2degC overnight. Leaves everywhere as expected for October (oct28). Birds are attracted to feeders in numbers, goldfinch, chaffinch and tits. A few fieldfares were feeding on berries by the lane.

Oct 27

Oct 29

Oct 30

Oct 29b

Oct 31

Oct 29 (8degC. Changeable)
5mm of rain since last reading. As the sun rose in the sky, a rainbow halo appeared around it (oct29b). After sunset a woodcock rested on the drive (oct29) and a full moon reflected in the still surface of the lake while tawny owls 'twit-tawooed' nearby.

Oct 30 (8degC. Sunny)
Flocks of redwings and fieldfares fed on hedgerow berries beside some bullfinches. green woodpeckers fighting on occasions. I spotted a couple of vapourer moths and a male common hawker along with female brown hawker laying eggs in the lake side marginals. Sparrowhawk, buzzard and long tailed tits also noted. Berries still holding on (oct30).

Oct 31 (11degC. Fine)
While clearing some of the fallen Oak branch I found a millipede (oct31) under some bark. Quite breezy which has stripped some leaves from the trees.

November

Nov 3

Nov 01 (7degC. Rain/wind. SR-06.52hrs SS-16.37)
Very wet now and lake approaching half way up the pipe. A buzzard and a kestrel got chased away by the crows this morning. After clearing weeds near the owl oak, I noticed these plump toadstools (nov1).

Nov 02 (8degC. Sun/showers)
First short fishing session for a while proved difficult to eventually catch a small common carp about half a pound. This fell to soft hooker pellet after blanking on sweetcorn/hemp pellet. A while later at a different peg I caught a nice common about 8lb (nov2b), consider that the net is 21 inches across. A couple of large frogs (nov2) escaped shelter as I weeded under rose bushes.

Nov 03 (7degC. Windy)
A shower but mainly fair day. Many pheasants accumulating along with twenty or thirty partridge. A harlequin ladybirds (nov3) sought shelter behind a dead leaf.

Nov 04 (6degC. Rain)
10mm rain recorded, mostly in last 24 hours. Just when I thought I wouldn't get a photo today, a flight of swans (nov4) flew over, possibly hoopers. Lake clearing a lot now possible to see the fish easily at feeding time and admire their size, although they are very reluctant to feed off the surface now. Very dull day.

Nov 2b

Nov 1

Nov 4

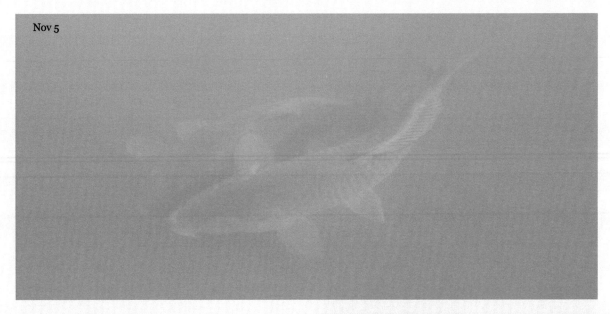

Nov 05 (8degC. Fine)
Fish look great 1 the clearing water (nov5).
Barn owl hunted at sunset.
Nov 06 (8degC. Fine/rain)
2degC. overnight and frost (nov6), sunny
morning. Lots of cock pheasants and fieldfares.
Nov 07 (9degC. Fine)
A couple of ommon darters showed in the
morning sun after a roe deer tip toed across
the field near the lake. Tawny owl called last
night and woodpeckers, buzzard and wren also
spotted. A few caddis flies seemed to be hatching
from the water too. Autumn colours (nov7) but
still lots of green leaves.

Nov 6

Nov 7

Nov 8

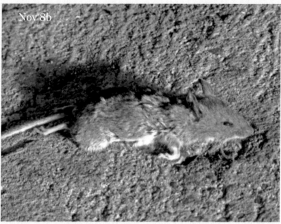

Nov 8b

Nov 9

Nov 08 (10degC. fine)
I trod on a large house mouse (nov8b) outside the front door this morning kindly left there for me by Ziggy I suspect. Inspired by the bugs around the outside light last night, I set the moth trap and caught two moths, one of which was a feathered thorn (nov8). Masses of crows about and sometimes they mobbed a passing buzzard.

Nov 09 (10degC. fine)
While building a bonfire, I heard something moving behind me. After a while a noticed a weasel, it leapt across the meadow's fallen long grasses and when it saw me It sat upright proudly holding a vole in its jaws (no camera!). The yellow Buddleia at the lake side is still blooming (nov9).

Nov 10 (10degC. fine/drizzle)
Wet start but good sunset. Moles (nov10) are loving the wet ground. Gnats swarmed at dusk.

Nov 10

Nov 11

Nov 12

Nov 13

Nov 13a

Nov 11 (8degC. sunny)
Several pheasants about often cocks and hens are separate. Berries still prevail (nov11).
Nov 12 (10degC. Wet)
2mm of rain since Nov 09. Frosty again this morning. The wet night brought out a toad (nov12) and a crested newt (and worms).
Nov 13 (12degC. fine)
Fieldfares at a distance (nov13a). Candlesnuff fungus in the cover belt (nov13).

Nov 14

Nov 15

Nov 15b

Nov 15c

Nov 14 (12degC. Fine)
3mm of rain since 12th. Fine and mild day, pity I was at work and missed it. As the sun set, the mist rose from the ground till quite dense (nov14).

Nov 15 (11degC. Foggy)
Calm day shattered by the drone of nearby tractor ploughing. Everything dripping wet (nov15). Male winter moth (nov15b) on the front door all night until morning! The female of the winter moth is flightless, I haven't seen one this winter yet. Unusual shaped wood blewit mushroom (nov15c).

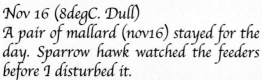

Nov 16 (8degC. Dull)
A pair of mallard (nov16) stayed for the day. Sparrow hawk watched the feeders before I disturbed it.

Nov 17 (8degC. Showers)
Last night an otter killed one of the biggest common carp (nov17) about 8lb, then to just take one bite! Nightly patrols seem useful now. After dark, on otter patrol, I think I saw a water vole. A 'plop' and something swam underwater to a grassy clump which I later spied a tiny pair of eyes watching me through the glare of the torchlight, and then turning to hide.

Nov 18 (8degC. sunny)
Frosty night leaving a thin icy section on the lake. Buzzard, woodpeckers, redwing, song thrush (nov18b) and coal tit (nov18a) showed. Long tailed tits (nov18c) flitted about in small flocks.

Nov 19

Nov 19 (10degC. fine)
Leaves built up (nov19) on water as the breeze strengthened. No sign of otter again last night. I found time to dispose of the dead fish, now nibbled by rats and magpies (nov19b).

Nov 20 (11degC. windy & dull)
Three roe deer (nov20) camped in the garden overnight near the orchard. About 1mm of rain last night which was a mild 10degC.

Nov 21 (10degC. drizzle)
Barn owl (nov21) braved the wet for a leisurely hunt this morning and evidence that he/she may have been in the cart lodge overnight too, by the white splashes of poo on the floor.

Nov 19b

Nov 21

Nov 20

Nov 22

Nov 23a

Nov 23

Nov 23b

Nov 22 (11degC. windy)

5mm of rain since yesterday. Several fieldfares in far oak (nov22) and both buzzard and bullfinch heard but not seen. Two large geese flew over no i.d.

Nov 23 (8degC. sunny)

7mm more rain overnight. The morning sky was divided into two halves: cloudy & clear blue (nov23b). For several hours the cloud margin slid across the sky until it cleared all together. I spied a large bird that I assumed to be a buzzard being mobbed by crows around 09.00hrs and noticed something hanging down from its body. I first assumed it was a tail feather but a later sighting around 11.00hrs proved it to be jesses (nov23a). I then reported it to a falconry 'lost & found' register and identified it as a Goshawk (nov23).

Nov 24

Nov 24a

Nov 24c

Nov 24 (6degC. Showers)
1degC. overnight but calm. Misty start (nov24b). Drizzle by midday and breeze picking up.
Sweet high pitched chirruping lead to a sighting of the tiny goldcrest in the weeping birch tree.
One at a time, six or more blue tits (nov24) were feeding on the bird table along with collard
doves (nov24c) while nearby, a male Spotted woodpecker (nov24a) also fed.

Nov 24b

Nov 25 (8degC. Gales)

11mm since yesterday. Generally fine and wind dropped late p.m. barn owl hunted at dusk. Mr (or Mrs) Robin fed on scraps of food from the other birds messy feeding (nov25).

Nov 26 (9degC. fine)

3mm in the rain gauge and lake now over half way up the pipe. A new species of fungi: white saddle, (nov26b) is growing under hazel at the lake edge. A brambling mixed with greenfinches and goldfinches on the feeder (nov26) and a few chaffinches too. While fishing this afternoon, without my camera, a cock bullfinch fed on bramble and a little owl (nov26a) stayed long enough for me to get the camera. At least three tawny owls and a two little owls were calling after dark (overcast but moonlit night).

Nov 27 (8degC. Showers)

3mm of rain. Windy and wet again. coal tit zoomed in and out from the feeders (nov27) tricky to get a photo, poor light and taken through double glazing didn't help.

Nov 28

Nov 29a

Nov 28 (6degC. Showers)
1mm of rain. Full moon last night illuminated everywhere like daylight. Two barn owls (nov28) hunted at sunset.

Nov 29

Nov 30

Nov 29 (4degC. Changeable)
Small groups of cramp ball fungus on Oak twigs (nov29). A short fishing session before sunset fishing maggot a float I caught a few small carp and perch then finally a 2lb 7oz Perch (nov29a).
Nov 30 (2degC. Sunny)
0degC. last night so a white frost (nov30) everywhere which stayed in shaded areas. Coal tit was about again. Lots of finches fed at times during the day, even a robin tried hanging on to the feeders.

December

Dec 01 (3degC. Showers. SR- 07.31hrs SS – 15.58hrs)

Very cold and breezy after 3mm of rain early a.m. Otter spotted on the lake after 23.30hrs and evidence of it came to light this morning as a few small scraps of fish in the reeds. Hundreds of birds, Flocks of Fieldfares and Redwings (dec1b), a few Starlings and many finches. Barn owl about at 15.00hrs. Lake level up beyond halfway up the pipe (dec1) and King's pond is virtually full (dec1c).

Dec 02 (2degC. Sunny)

Below freezing last night. White frost about all day despite blue skies. Ice on the lake expanding as sun set (dec2).

Dec 03 (6degC. Showers)

5mm of rain. Minus 1degC overnight rising quickly after sunrise. Rain early morning. Blossom on a garden shrub (dec3).

Dec 04 (5degC. Drizzle)

Trumpet-like lichens (dec4) grow amongst the moss on an old tree trunk.

Dec 05 (5degC. Fine)

Snow and sleet last night accumulated 3mm in the rain gauge. (dec5).

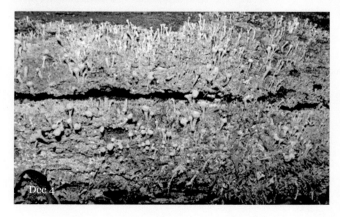

Dec 6a

Dec 6b

Dec 06 (4degC. Fine)
A dusting of snow last night. The tree surgeons arrived this morning to cut the alders on the long drive. Possibly hundreds of redwings and fieldfares. Bird table and feeders were busy. (dec6b) Blackbird, song thrush, great tit, blue tit, chaffinch, bullfinch, goldfinch, greenfinch, robin, dunnock, greater spotted woodpecker, collard dove and moorhen all had a meal. I startled a brown hare at the field margin and it reacted strangely by standing upright (dec6a) for several seconds more than once.

Dec 07 (3degC. Showers)
12mm of rain in 24hrs. Snow and sleet early a.m. Lake level is up (dec7) near the top of the pipe. A sparrowhawk swooped across the drive towards the garden in the afternoon as the wind increased it seemed much colder.

Dec 7

Dec 08 (4degC. Fine)
Foggy for an hour or so mid morning then sunny. Ditch is almost full now (dec8) as the lake overflows into it. Water very clear indicating that the fish are dormant. Some lapwings flew over as barn owl hunted near sunset. We are now full circle into winter again, as tens of fieldfares fed on the remaining berries (dec8a) outside my window.

Dec 9

Dec 09 (6degC. Windy)
2mm in the rain gauge since 07. Fieldfares along with blackbirds continue to raid the berries in numbers. Windy and high water (dec09).

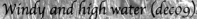

Dec 8

Dec 8a

Dec 11

Dec 12

Dec 12a

Dec 10b

Dec 10 (4degC. Drizzle)
Hundreds of crows flocked in search for food (dec10), water in the ditch by the public footpath is high (dec10b); only a few inches from the plank bridge.

Dec 11 (0degC. Foggy)
A few Siskins (dec11) and a yellowhammer (dec11a) arrived today also a hen brambling. Mainly foggy but some sunny intervals made up for the bitter cold.

Dec 12 (0degC. freezing fog)
-2degC overnight. Fog cleared at sunrise but frost only thawed from some trees during the day (dec12). A spooky tinkling sound of the ice falling onto the iced lake was interesting (dec12b). A few siskins and a snipe spotted later, identified only by its zig-zag flight. A hare (dec12a) hopped towards me until it was about to sniff my boots then decided to hop away leisurely.

Dec 11a

Dec 12b

Dec 13a

Dec 14

Dec 13b

Dec 15c

Dec 15a

15-Dec-12 13:16

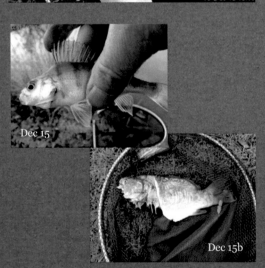
Dec 15

Dec 15b

Dec 13 (0degC. fine)
-3degC overnight. A young (ringed) black headed gull was eating a piece of bread on the lake this morning (dec13a). And lots of fieldfares feasted on fallen berries (dec13b).

Dec 14 (6degC. Windy/Rain)
Despite 7mm of rainfall, the lake is still ice covered. A very dark and wet day, (dec14) certainly didn't feel 'mild'. The tall leaning Eucalyptus was removed today as the tree fellers completed their work.

Dec 15 (6degC. Mainly fine)
Otter killed at least two fish last night judging by the remains I found this morning, one mirror carp about 4 lb (dec15b) and a common about 2 lb. I watched the barn owl while fishing this afternoon and caught a nice common at 8lb (dec15a) showing some scars from escaping the otter's clutch, and a few small perch (dec15). Several lapwings flew over amongst hundreds of crows. Ditch is full (dec15c) so I won't be using the stepping stones. I drove to the village shop after dark and saw 20-30 winter moths, the most I have seen.

Dec 16

Dec 17a
Dec 16a
Dec 18
Dec 20

Dec 17b

Dec 19

Dec 18a

Dec 16 (7degC. Sunny)

Sparrowhawk and kestrel (dec16) both showed and barn owl hunted just before sunset as usual, resting close to me as I grabbed some fishing time. I caught a nice mirror carp at 8 lb which was '010' (dec16a) on my list which showed it has gained at least 1 lb per year since 2007.

Dec 17 (7degC. Fine)

Frost early and moon was out today (dec17). The small hedgehog (dec17a) I found in the rat trap cage, yesterday, was no better today and sadly the vet said it needed putting down. I found several pairs of mating winter moths on the wheelie bin (dec17b), normal place to find them easily.

Dec 18 (6degC. Fine)

A pair of Mallard (dec18) was on the lake at first light, they took off as I got closer. When I refilled the bird feeders I noticed a treecreeper clinging to the barn wall. I had walked past it twice before I snapped this close-up shot (dec18a).

Dec 19 (6degC. Overcast)

Pretty spider: some kind of harvestman (dec19) skulking on a Field maple, looks like eggs nearby. Fish have been feeding well but at least two more lost to the otter.

Dec 20 (7degC. Rain)

9mm of rain. What can I say? Wet? Hundreds of crows (dec20) everywhere but returning to feed on stubble field.

Dec 21

Dec 23

Dec 22b

Dec 21 (9degC. Fine)

3mm more rain in the gauge and ditch and moat are quite full (dec21). Winter cherry trees are blossoming but too wet for spring bulbs I reckon.

Dec 22 (8degC. Rain)

12mm of rain. This morning I looked out of the window and spotted a fox on the other side of the lake and managed to grab the camera and swap the lens for the big zoom. I then ran outside in the rain and got a few shots but this (dec22) is the best, it appeared to be carrying a moorhen. During the following chase I saw a couple of pairs of Bullfinches (dec22b) although I couldn't get close enough for a good photo.

Dec 23 (10degC. Windy)

Another 7mm of rain overnight. Ditches by the road, the lane (dec23), field side and over the lake are all full. Moat is full too. Several long tailed tits and a few fieldfares showed along with green woodpecker.

Dec 22

Dec 24

Dec 26

Dec 24a

Dec 26b

Dec 24 (11degC. Rain)

11mm of rain mostly overnight. Moat is near the point of overflow and lake is just over the top of the pipe. Winter cherry trees are pretty (dec24a). More fungi on Elder (dec24).

Dec 25 (8degC. Showers)

3mm of rain overnight. A sparrowhawk (dec25) was sitting on the bird table in the morning.

Dec 26 (7degC. Sun/shower)

Several late trooping funnel toadstools were growing near an Oak over the hay field. They were mostly about 20cm across (dec26). I also spotted a pair of reed buntings (male dec26b).

Dec 25

Dec 29a

Dec 27 (6degC. Rain.)
13mm of rain. I found the large tench dismembered by the lake (dec27) so I guess the otter came back last night. Moat is now brimming and path-bridge is floating.
Dec 28 (10degC. Fair. Full moon)
3mm more rain. King's pond is quite full (dec28).
Dec 29 (10degC. Wind/showers)
The small hay field 'dip' is water logged (dec29a) I think this is the first time I have seen water laying there to this extent. Still some candle snuff fungi near the meadow (dec29).

Dec 28

Dec 27

Dec 29

Dec 30a

Dec 30 (7degC. Mainly Sunny)
A weasel scurried around King's pond but no chance of a photo. Feeders were very busy (dec30) and Crows still gathering in flocks on the maize (dec30a).

Dec 31 (9degC. Windy)
2mm more rain since Dec 28. 4degC last night and overcast and dull now (dec31).

Dec 30

Dec 31

temperature & rainfall 2012

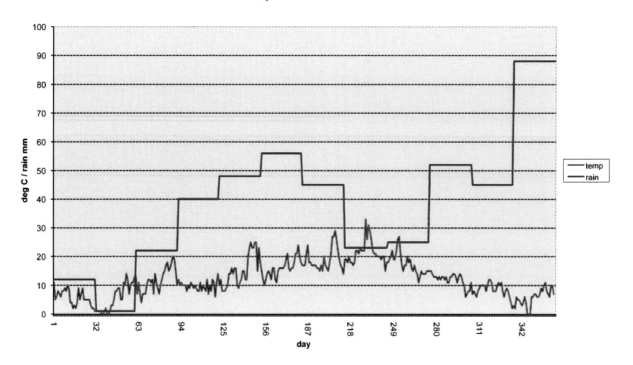

Nature Signs

		2008	2009	2010	2011	2012	2013
first	newt		Feb-18	Mar-17	Jan-14	Feb-24	Mar-05
last			Nov-03	Nov-14	Dec-21	Oct-04	
first	frog		Mar-14	Mar-24	Feb-14	Mar-03	
last					Nov-24	Oct-25	
first	toad	Mar-27	Feb-23	Mar-18	Feb-10	Mar-10	Mar-06
	spawn	Apr-04	Mar-31	Mar-23	Mar-22	Mar-16	
	toad count		135	500	260	200	
	fish spawning	May-08	May-21	May-16	(may-01)	May-24	
					(jun-15)		
first	swallow		Mar-30	Apr-17	Mar-27	Apr-14	
last				Sep-10	Sep-18	Oct-04	
first	martin			Jun-04	x	x	
last				Sep-04	x	x	
	bee		Feb-21	Mar-23	Feb-22	Mar-08	Feb-17
	crocus			Mar-08	Feb-07	Feb-18	Mar-02
	daffodil				Mar-10	Mar-08	
	may			May-18	Apr-20	May-11	
	catkins				Feb-10	Jan-10	Feb-16
	pussy willow			Mar-08	Feb-25	Mar-01	Feb-22
	cuckoo			May-04	Apr-21	Apr-27	

Technical details: cameras include Canon 550D, with Tamron 90mm macro, Canon 80-200mm & Sigma 150-500mm. Panasonic FZ18, Sony Ericson K800